Contents

Page 4	Foreword	
Page 5	Introduction	
Page 6	Chapter One	How it all Began (1774-1819)
Page 21	Chapter Two	The Construction of the Canal
Page 26	Chapter Three	The Route of the Canal and its Unique Features
Page 32	Chapter Four	The Canal's Decline and Demise
Page 39	Chapter Five	The Passing of a Great Engineering Enterprise and the Creation of a Water Supply for Stratton & Bude
Page 42	Chapter Six	Life on the Canal Part I
Page 48	Chapter Seven	Life on the Canal Part II
Page 53	Chapter Eight	The Twilight Years
Page 57	Chapter Nine	The Present State of the Canal
Page 65	Chapter Ten	Into the Millennium
Page 67	Chapter Eleven	The Regeneration Project
Page 76	Appendix I	Viewing Points
Page 78	Appendix II	Ships Built at Bude
Page 80	Appendix III	Summary of Facts

Foreword

by Neil H Burden chair of the Bude Canal Regeneration Partnership

This book records the detailed history of the Bude Canal up to spring 2009. It has been reprinted in celebration of the completion of the regeneration of the Bude Canal which was instigated and delivered by North Cornwall District Council (NCDC).

On behalf of all those involved in this mammoth task I would like to give particular credit to the Bude Canal and Harbour Society and the Bude Canal Trust who by their very knowledge and enthusiasm and being enthralled by this engineering feat, mostly carried out by manual labour, encouraged the district council to take a lead. As a consequence the Council, with 3 other principle funders and the support of the members and officers of NCDC, restored facets of the barge and tub canal which had not been in working order for over 80 years.

I would like to pay tribute to the writers of the first 10 chapters which were published in an earlier book by Bryan Dudley Stamp and Bill Young and which sets the scene of what must have been a great activity in the late Georgian and early Victorian times.

Charlie David, who has been the lead officer on the regeneration project for many years, has put together in the final chapter a record of the events over the last few years. The results of this project can only be described as a regenerated canal for the enjoyment of a very wide cross section of local people and visitors alike for a great many years to come.

I was reported in the press some while back as saying the canal was leaking like a colander, that banks were breaking down, the locks were walled up and that there was much silting up from Helebridge to Whalesborough Lock as well as in the Bude Basin itself. I stated that this was why we needed to act swiftly as time was running out for the canal and its future existence. These, and many other issues, we have now been able to address.

In the following pages you can read the detail of how the work progressed, which together with the treasured old photos and records provides an excellent case history. The use of modern digital photography now shows in detail the areas of the recent restoration.

I take this opportunity to sincerely thank the funders, the public's forbearance during the project implementation and especially the members of the Bude Canal Regeneration Partnership and its Steering Group for their loyalty and support over the past 10 years. It has been good that so many of us have stayed the course and have seen the project completed.

Neil Burden, March 2009

Introduction

Most of the books on the "Bude Canal" are out-of-date or simply out of print. But lately there appears to be a resurgence of interest in the Canal, particularly after the formation of the Bude Canal Society and latterly the Bude Canal Trust Ltd, and also the fact that local schools are still setting essays and projects on this fascinating and unique West Country engineering enterprise. Nationally and in the County of Cornwall especially, all things Cornish that are part of our heritage and distinguished past are of great significance in these days of advanced technology and the awesome unpredictability of the future. The authors have recently published a book "Bude, Past and Present" with only a small chapter devoted to the Bude Canal, but a kind donation from the Bude Canal Trust Social Section, and the fact that a small market now exists for this book, has given a "kick-start" to this new publication.

Bryan Stamp (with Rennie Bere) in 1980 published "The Book of Bude and Stratton", which traced the growth and roots of the towns and their surrounding countryside "to the delight and instruction of resident and visitor alike". Bill Young issued his own account (and history) of his walk down the whole length of the canal, "Walking along the Old Bude Canal". He has led parties down the underground wheel pits, and led walks on various stretches of the delightful towpaths, and, together with John Street, produced an enjoyable video that highlighted the unrivalled features on every branch of the Canal. Nevertheless, none of this research would have been possible without the use of maps, articles and books written by Monica Ellis, Helen Harris, and Joan Rendell, who very kindly allowed us to use, and have access to, their books and photographs. We are deeply grateful for their unstinting help over many years which will allow us to perpetuate the interest that they have undoubtedly generated in the hearts and minds of past and present generations. We are also greatly indebted to the curators of the Town museum who gave us access to their large collection of slides. We trust that we are worthy successors to a long line of historians and writers, dealing with all aspects of the canal, and that the book is a creditable tribute to the tireless and hardworking men who for many years succeeded in making this venture the enterprise it certainly was.

We make no apologies for reprinting old photographs of the many ships in harbour but the names and captains will add interest to this unique record.

CHAPTER 1

How it all Began (1774-1819)

Early Proposals, Reports and Surveys

The first proposal for a Bude Canal was put forward early in 1774. It was projected by John Edyvean who was at the time pioneering the St Columb Canal in Cornwall.

A route for the canal was surveyed by Edmund Leach and John Box before the first meeting in February 1774. Box and Leach said that the canal would be "of great public utility".

Edyvean, Leach and Box were called to give evidence before the House of Lords Committee before being given consideration to the Bill. The landlords concerned and seven of the county's JPs (Justice of the Peace) signified their approval. The Bill "An Act for making a navigable Cut or Canal from the Port or Harbour of Bude, in the hundred of Stratton, in the county of Cornwall, to the River Tamar, in the parish of Calstock, in the said county" - was passed, receiving the Royal Assent on 24th May, 1774.

The canal was meant to link the Bristol and English Channels by way of the Tamar's navigable waterway.

It was proposed that not only Bude sand, but also Welsh coal, limestone and other manures, timber, mining products, agricultural goods and domestic supplies, would all be transported on this system.

The direct distance between Bude and Calstock is appropriately 28 miles, but the proposed canal was to follow a route that extended to almost 90 miles. It was to pass through Marhamchurch, Poundstock, Whitstone, Bridgerule, North Tamerton, Boyton, Werrington, North Petherwin, Tremaine and Egloskerry, to Launceston; and from there by way of Laneast, Lewannick, North Hill, Linkinhorne and Stoke Climsland to Calstock.

The long route had to be taken due to the features of the countryside. A clause in the Act said that the cutting on the canal's lower side could not be more than 39 inches deep. This, however, was not considered to be a disadvantage as a maximum number of parishes and outlying farms would be served with the sand.

The canal was to have a width of 21 feet at the top and 12 feet at the bottom and was to be deep enough to handle tub-boats of 10 tons. The land used - including towing paths which were to be fenced (except where boats were to pass each other, or to be turned or docked) - was not to exceed 53 feet in width.

Another clause in the Act stated that near the Whiteford mansion (Stoke Climsland) the canal should be arched over and carried underground for a distance of 300 feet.

The canal needed to be raised above the terminal points to pass over the hilly country; it was proposed to do this by means of five 'Inclined Planes', using engines apparently invented by Edyvean himself. The planes were capable of using trucks, and so cargoes had to be transferred at each plane.

The summit level was to run for a distance of 68 miles.

Three of the inclined planes were to be at the Bude end and two were to be used to take the canal down to connect with the Tamar. The first plane was to have a 54ft rise, the second - $6^{1}/_{2}$ miles further along - 120ft rise, the third - 4 miles on - 66ft rise. The summit was, therefore, 240ft above sea level.

The two planes at the Tamar end were to be a 120ft drop each. The first drop was at a point $2^{1}/_{2}$ miles from the Tamarside terminus, where the fifth inclined plane was to be sited, at Kelly Rock, Calstock.

The raising of the £40,000 capital, needed in £100 shares was authorised and various local people gave their support, notably Sir John Molesworth and the Call and Rodd families. Twenty thousand pounds extra was available if required. The limit was twenty shares per person, with each person able to vote once for each share they held.

The first breakwater - drawing by Sir Thomas Acland

Payment for use of the canal was free, except for the rate on the goods transported:

Per ton of: slate, stone, sand, culm, coals, timber and manure - not to exceed 2s 0d.

Per ton of: goods, wares or merchandise - not to exceed 3s 0d.

No wharfage was to be charged for goods remaining at the wharves for less than 24 hours and only 2d or 3d per ton for that remaining a week.

The commissioners were empowered to raise or lower tolls at their discretion, provided that the shareholders received interest at 6%.

Due to the unattractive financial prospects from the low rates of Tolls on the canal and the limited amount of authorised capital, work was not started. By the following year there was talk of abandoning the project.

Smeaton's suggestion for locks and dams

John Smeaton (1724-92) was an engineer who was famous for the reconstruction of the Eddystone Lighthouse and for planning a route for the Forth and Clyde Canal. In 1777 he was consulted on the practicability of the Bude canal scheme. He walked the proposed lines and had no doubt that it was practicable, but he estimated the cost at £119,201 and was very concerned about the economics of it all.

Smeaton remarked, "the county of Cornwall .... seems but ill-adapted for the making of canals across the country, being so very frequently intersected with valleys, that to preserve a level for any considerable space between two given points, it became necessary to go through a vast meandering course".

In his report to the promoters, dated 8th January 1778, Smeaton considered various modifications and alternative ideas, estimating the cost of each and the respective financial returns which could be expected. One of the suggestions was for shortening the proposed length by altering the planned route between Bude and Launceston and carrying it over Greena Moor (1 mile SE of Week St Mary). This would have reduced its length by 15 miles and would have avoided several small valleys.

Smeaton, while observing the valley of the River Tamar, noticed how easily the river above Calstock could be adopted as a navigable

The forge on the sand wharf.

waterway by means of locks and dams. He therefore prepared another scheme. He suggested that six locks should be built in the Bude River Neet to make it navigable for 3½ miles upstream, then 6 miles of canal constructed, rising by two inclined planes to the summit level, and another inclined plane to bring the canal down to join the Tamar near North Tamerton. He remarked that from here, ten or more locks would be needed to take the canal to Greystone Bridge - 15½ miles beyond. There was a possibility of a branch up the tributary River Kensey to Launceston.

Smeaton estimated the cost from Bude to Greystone Bridge at £46,109. He made no estimates for continuing the waterway to Calstock, although he was sure this could be done for less money by locking the river. His report, however, was disregarded; no start was made and the scheme was abandoned in 1784.

Leach's idea for Inclined Planes

In 1785 Edmund Leach made an attempt to revive interest in the Bude Canal. Leach provided some new ideas based mainly on Smeaton's reports. He put these forward in a book called 'A Treatise of Universal Inland Navigation'.

Leach was obviously fascinated by the inclined planes and their uses. These had only been used on the Tyrone canal in Ireland so far. He

A unique photograph of the long barges - with the schooner "Annie Davey"

considered these to be less expensive than the locks that Smeaton had suggested. Leach drew up a new plan for the canal, shortening the route and using inclined planes to raise the tub boats.

He proposed to take the route from Bude Haven up the valley, possibly with a branch to Widemouth. It was to have an inclined plane to the cliff top at Bude and at Widemouth. There was to be an inclined plane at the foot of Week St Mary Hill to raise the boats and their cargoes to the 9½ mile "Canal of Partition". This would travel along Week St Mary valley to Whitstone and a place called "Pack-Saddle".

Here it would receive a supply of water from the Tamar by an aqueduct from Shernick Moor (north of Bridgerule). It would then descend down into the Tamar Valley near the stretch to Calstock. Leach used the idea of a side-canal, with another inclined plane instead of river navigation and locks.

The cost of the whole scheme, 40¾ miles from Bude to Calstock, was put at £53,100 by Leach. This was a considerable saving on the estimate of £88,740 in 1774.

Leach put forward a design for a "mechanical hydraulic machine" for use on the inclined planes and which could be adapted for use on canals or in mines. Leach opposed Edyvean's idea of reloading cargoes at each ascent and descent and planned to carry the boats along the whole canal without unloading. He recommended using oak or other wood for construction of the line of the plane between two levels. It was to be (for canals) 22ft 6in in breadth and divided longitudinally into equal parts with wooden ledges along the sides and along the middle. The path on each side was to be 10 feet wide. A strong wall (with sluices) would be required at the end of the upper canal section and between this and the head of the plane a horizontal platform of two equal parts would be required. There were to be rollers on the canal side of the wall to allow the boats to pass in and out and further sluices to allow water to be let out to power a water wheel.

Special vehicles were to transfer the boats and their cargoes up and down the paths. These were roughly triangular in section and were designed to carry the boats horizontally. There was a cistern which contained water for use as a counter-balance.

There were rollers between the bottom of the vehicle and the plane, these were for the vehicle to rest on, therefore it could be easily transferred to and from the canal.

Tub boats in the lower canal basin

How it all Began (1774-1819)

There was a hole in the bottom of the cistern to allow water to enter and the vehicle to sink below water-level when taking on boats from the canal's lower section. This ballast water was to be allowed to discharge as the vehicle ascended the plane (this was to effect correct balance with its descending twin). Operation was partly by counter-balance and partly by power from the waterwheel.

However, the canal still remained unbuilt in spite of the ingenuity of the plans.

The Nuttall's Report

In the early 1790's there was again renewed interest in the Bude Canal. This was about the time when a new ambitious scheme was being planned for the construction of a 30 mile canal from Morwellham on the river Tamar to Tamerton Bridge.

Early in 1793 a canal from Bude through Holsworthy to Hatherleigh was considered. The survey was made by Bentley and Bolton. A sum of money £10,480) was subscribed by such people as Sir William Molesworth, Sir John Call, Denys Rolle and the Cohans. In July 1793 Bentley and Bolton were commissioned to make a detailed survey, but they were too busy with other

Ladies out for a walk at Rodd's Bridge

jobs and two engineers, John and George Nuttall, took over. Their report was presented to a meeting held in the White Hart Inn, Holsworthy, on 25th October 1793, with Lord Stanhope in the chair.

The Nuttall's reported that the canal would have to be carried at a height of 473½ft to cross the easternmost ridge by means of an 11ft cutting at Hammetts Lane (north-east of Holsworthy). They also considered the methods by which they could lift the canal. Steam engines and perpendicular lifts were rejected, so was the system of ropes and Whimseys (sheer legs and pully blocks) powered by horses or steam. Locks were also ruled out due to the potential insufficiency of water for the number of locks required; also because of the time needed to pass a boat and its cargo through the lock; and also if the locks were made big enough to take the maximum cargo load, the cost would be too great. Locks it was thought, would also deprive mills in the district of their supplies of water.

The Nuttall's favoured the use of 'iron-rail roads' laid on the planes in conjunction with the canal. They found that it would be possible to construct the canal in four level sections and to connect them by lengths of railway (this amounted to almost 4 miles of railway in all). The first length of ¼ mile was to be at Bude. This would rise to the canal's first level section which was 2½ miles long. It would take the route into Stratton Valley - north of Marhamchurch. The second length of railway was to be here - about 2¼ miles long - which was to run up the Cann Orchard valley and eastwards south of Thorn, it was to travel for 8¼ miles and pass under the Launceston to Kilkhampton road by way of a ¾ mile tunnel. It was then to proceed in a curving pattern to the bank of the Tamar at Burmsdon. There was also to be a branch from a point near Thorn to run southwards towards Merrifield and continue to Tamerton Bridge. Here there was to be a double inclined plane so that a connection could be made with any canal constructed northwards from Launceston.

From Burmsdon there was to be a third length of railway, just over 1¼ miles long. It was to ascend through Pancrasweek to Lana, here there would be a connection with the canal's summit level. The principal level section was to be at least 50 miles in length. There was to be a short side branch near the start northwards to Wood - this was to be a branch to meet a sand road that passed between Virworthy and Lutton. The

Rodd's Bridge - the barge section of the canal

How it all Began (1774-1819)

summit level was to run eastwards over Ugworthy Moor and to bend south over Manworthy Moor to a field near Hammetts Lane, from there over Blagdon Moor by Launceston and Herdwick. East of Holsworthy the canal would cross the Hatherleigh road and then run southwards to the head of the Claw Valley on Dunsland Moor. Here it was to meet the main road from Okehampton. There was to be another branch from Hammetts Lane to run north-eastwards to north of Woodacott, then westwards below Thuborough to Waterland Mill, Bradworthy (at this point it would be near the River Waldron). The Waldron was considered to be the best water supply for the canal, making it unnecessary to draw water from the Tamar.

There were to be four other tunnels in addition to the one at Thorn. They were to be at Bude (the canal's lowest reach); south of Holsworthy (east of Chasty); north of Woodacott and south of East Wonford. The tunnel north of Woodacott was to be the longest - nearly $\frac{1}{2}$ mile long, while the other three were to be under $\frac{1}{4}$ mile.

In order to continue the canal towards Hatherleigh and to circumnavigate the River Torridge, it was planned to cross the River Waldron near Waterland and to carry the canal eastwards following the Waldron Valley, to below Sutcombe in the Milton Damerel parish.

The summit level was to end here and there was to be a drop by means of

The ketch "Ceres" rounding Barrel Rock in rough seas

a double inclined plane down to the Torridge - which would be crossed just above Newton Mill, The fourth reach of the canal - of nearly 14 miles was to go on from here on the lower level below Allacott (in Shebbear Parish) to within a mile of Hatherleigh.

The estimate for the scheme from Bude (a 75 mile waterway) to Hatherleigh via Holsworthy, including five tunnels was £32,404. The Nuttall's also calculated that about 250,000 acres would benefit from the canal.

Lord Stanhope proposed to use small boats of 2 tons and to carry these on the rail sections suspended between a pair of wheels about 6ft in diameter. "Earl Stanhope ..... proposed ..... to have iron-rail roads of gradual and easy ascent, on which boats of two tons were to be used, suspended between a pair of wheels of about 6ft diameter and to be drawn up or let down the same by a horse. The meeting decided to seek an Act, and thanked Lord Stanhope for his indefatigable zeal and perseverance in pursuing and personally investigating the best means by which this great under-taking, so very beneficial to the adjacent county in particular and to the improvement of agriculture in Devon and Cornwall in general, might be accomplished, in spite of many natural difficulties not common to other counties."

The meeting at Holsworthy considered the Nuttall's report and resolved unanimously to apply for an Act.

Robert Fulton's idea for wheeled boats and water-powered inclined planes

In September of 1793 a three year correspondence began between Robert Fulton and Lord Stanhope. Fulton had suddenly been inspired concerning the design and engineering of inclined planes. His ideas were not entirely new, but they did have some say in how the planes should be built.

The first suggestion that Fulton made was for the working of the inclined planes by the use of water in containers to provide weight for descent. Lord Stanhope pointed out that this method had already been put forward by Edmund Leach. However, on the 8th May, 1794, Fulton obtained a patent for the use of a double inclined plane - using the water cistern (or caisson) arrangement. Each caisson was to be carried level on four or eight wheels. Fulton saw the plane as working by counter-balance, either the descending load would be heavier than that coming up, or additional water would be added to the descending caisson. Fulton provided for a capstan or waterwheel power to get the boats up the reverse slope from the upper pound of the carriage on which the boat is to float and be draw out of the canal, up the side-plane on the cistern ..... The power to drawn the boat on the cistern may be obtained by a capstan or a waterwheel.

The wooden boats were to be rectangular in shape, of 2-4ft width - the ones of 4ft width were recommended to be 20ft long and 2ft 10in deep. This would give a capacity of 4 tons. The two pairs of wheels underneath were to be from 6-10in in diameter, each pair being made in one piece with the axle.

In a book published in 1796, 'Treatise on Canal Navigation', Fulton further expounded his proposals for narrow canals and inclined planes and the use of shallow rectangular boats with wheels, but advocated alternative methods of lifting. One of these was for using power produced by a water tub descending in a perpendicular shaft to raise the loaded boats up the incline. The boats were to be attached by an individual chain to an endless chain that passed up one track of the double inclined plane and down the other and around wheels at the top and bottom. For planes of small ascent there was to be a waterwheel sited beside the top of the plane, instead of the descending tub, for providing the lifting and braking power.

These plans of Fulton's are very interesting because of their application in the building of the Bude Canal a quarter of a century later.

For the bucket-in-the-well system - the principle of which the Hobbacott plane later operated - Fulton advised, for the sake of economy, making a plane between selected hillside points that would provide the greatest possible rise at one time. Fulton explained that the slope of the hill should

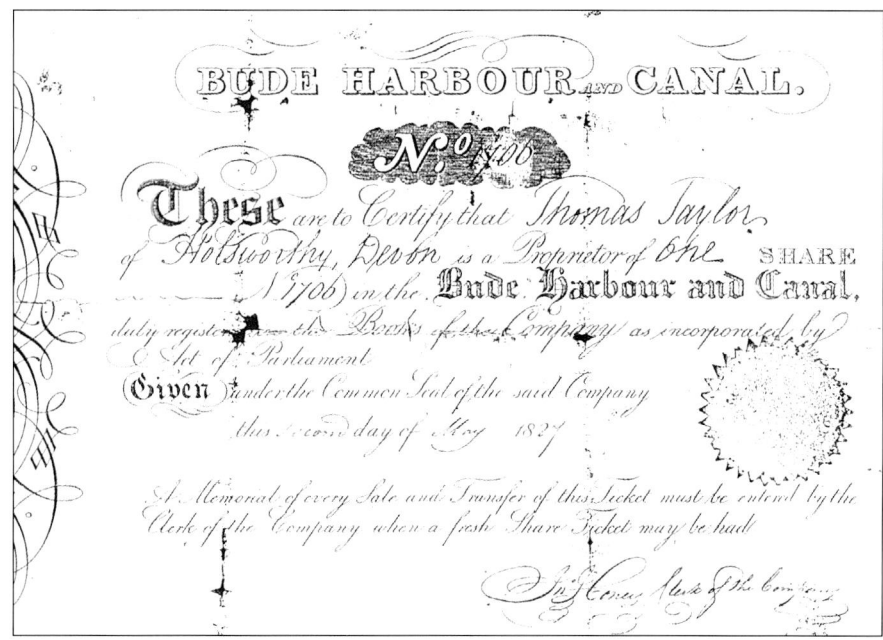

A company share certificate made out to Thomas Taylor of Holsworthy 1827

be formed into a regular incline between the canal's two water levels, at an angle less than 45 degrees. On this, the two planes each of 2ft 1 in width, made parallel, 6ft apart, would be placed. The iron rails were to be set on a bed of rubble overlaid with either coping stones or timber. The bottom of the plane was required to level out to a more gradual slope for a distance of about 60ft to the lower canal, with the track meeting the water, both here and at the top, by a gentle curved bridge, so as to prevent the undersides of the boats scraping the planes.

The well was to be 10-11ft in diameter and at the top of the plane. It was to be of equal depth to the difference between the two levels of the canal, with a drainage pipe from its bottom connecting with the lower waterway. The bucket used was to have a capacity in excess of the required 10 tons of water and to be 9ft in diameter and 5 ft high. It was to be made of wood or sheet iron with a 12-18in hole in the bottom fitted with a valve device which would open and discharge the water as the hub struck the bottom of the pit. The water from the upper canal was to be used for the tub, which would be suspended by two or more chains from a drum wheel over the mouth of the well, with balance chains and a weight on the opposite side for returning the emptied tub to the top of the pit. A shaft would convey power from the drum to the upper wheel for the plane's main chain; this wheel, set at the same angle as the plane, was to be 8ft in diameter so that its extremities would come exactly opposite the centre of the two planes. The corresponding wheel at the bottom of the plane was to be the same size, but set horizontally. The power from the inclined wheel at the top was also to be used for drawing the boats out of the upper canal. Fulton estimated that passage over the plane would take as little as $1\frac{1}{2}$ minutes.

James Green's Plan

Plans for the Bude Canal were discarded during the Napoleonic Wars and it was not until 1814 that a new plan was devised.

There met on that fateful day in 1814 two yeoman landowners - Mr Harward of Tackbeare, Bridgerule and Mr Braddon of Newacott. Both men were distressed about the number of unemployed people in rural areas after the war.

Braddon had in his possession Nuttall's report on 1793 and both men decided that Harward should go and consult Lord Stanhope. Lord Stanhope pronounced himself fully in agreement and it was decided to hold a meeting in London with other influential and interested people the following winter. But Napoleon returned from Elba and the war restarted. In 1816 Lord Stanhope died and the plan could have died a natural death. However,

How it all Began (1774-1819)

Messrs Braddon and Harward were not defeated. They obtained local support of Mr George Call of Vacey, North Tamerton and others. Mr Harward then approached the new Lord Stanhope, who gave his full support. In 1817 the engineer James Green and surveyor Thomas Shearm were asked to survey a line.

Green's instructions were to direct his attentions to the opening of a communication between Bude and certain points in the interior, the arrangement of the line being left to his discretion and to survey the haven of Bude and report how far it was capable of improvement. The points in the interior at first specified were Thornbury, Holsworthy and as far eastwards as time would allow, and Tamerton Bridge to the south. Green was also asked to continue his inspection to Launceston from Tamerton Bridge after a meeting of the subscribers.

Green's report was presented to the subscribers on 14th April, 1818. He had two choices - either to construct a canal, or a railway. He considered the railway to be less suitable because of the nature of the soil and the rise of the ground. The following extract is taken from the report to the subscribers:

"If therefore, a canal be resolved on, it ought to be on a small and inexpensive scale; and some of the same reasons which operate against a canal on lock principles, form

The inset wheel of a tub boat, for use on the rails of the inclined planes

serious objections to the adoption of a railroad, inasmuch as 362 feet of the whole elevation between Bude and Holsworthy must be attained before it can reach the line of the Tamar, and that within the space of five miles and a half.

This elevation is nearly equal to $^5/_{10}$ of an inch to every linear yard, or 11 inches to every chain, supposing the ascent graduated throughout the whole length, which could not easily be accomplished; and when done, a horse would not draw, in regular work, more than two tons upwards, in which direction by far the greatest trade is to be expected; and although, on reaching the summit, the horses load might be increased, on the extended and more easy parts of the rail-road, yet the frequent changes and irregularities of conveyance would be objectionable in a general trade. The nature of the soil also, upon every point of the line, is such to render it peculiarly ill-suited to a rail-road."

A footbridge on Thorne Farm with the original cast iron supports. Note the slot down the middle for the tow-rope

Green also saw a canal with locks as useless, on account of the cost. He, therefore, recommended a small and inexpensive depth of water. He proposed boats of 5 tons each, four of which were to be drawn by one horse. The ascents were to be overcome by water-powered inclined planes. He estimated that the planes could be constructed at a third of the expense of locks, worked with one-third of the amount of water and saved more than four-fifths of the time of passage.

Green observed that the harbour had its drawbacks in its smallness and the difficulty of entry. He recommended that some protection for the strong seas and possible deepening of the harbour was needed. This could be done with a breakwater, 10ft above spring tide level, to be constructed to close the gap between the mainland and the Chapel Rocks. He also recommended that the channel of the river should be deepened to a point near the sandhills.

Although Green had also surveyed and estimated for a smaller length of canal, unconnected with the harbour and on the eastern side of the river he proposed to start the canal at the bend of the river with a lock capable of admitting vessels of 40-50 tons and to continue the line along the west side of the valley towards Helebridge - a distance of almost 2 miles. The channel was to be 24ft wide at the bottom, 37ft 6ins at the top and 4ft 6ins deep. Green planned to accomplish the 25ft rise by means of two more locks, (taking water from near Helebridge as a supply). Barges of 40 tons could navigate the canal at the foot of the first inclined plane, where the cargo could be transferred to the small boats. The locks could be used by four or six small boats at the same time if necessary. Green proposed that a later improvement scheme would be to construct a ship lock at the entrance to admit vessels of 70-100 tons into the basin - where there might be warehouses on the banks.

It was proposed to rise by inclined plane at Marhamchurch and Thurlibeer after Helebridge. The line as far as Burmsdon and North Tamerton was basically the same as that proposed by the Nuttalls, but at Burmsdon, Green proposed to construct an aqueduct to bridge the Tamar and then an inclined plane near Veala to take the canal to its summit level. He planned a branch at Virworthy to make sand available to the parishes of Sutcombe, Milton Damerel and Bradworthy and also to serve as a feeder for the canal's water supply. For the water supply he proposed a 60 acre reservoir at Alfardisworthy on the River Tamar.

The canal was to continue eastwards from Holsworthy via Dunsland Moor, Chilla and Northlew and continue to Brightley Bridge 1½ miles north of Okehampton on the Okement River. Here Green terminated his survey, although he was sure that the line could be continued to South Zeal, Bow

The upper reaches of the canal in water, some years ago

and Crediton, for communications with Exeter, Tiverton and various other important towns.

He planned to have one inclined plane descending from the summit level on the line to Tamerton Bridge.

Green stated that the total cost of construction and harbour improvements was estimated at £128,341. He estimated that an annual return on capital of at least 10% on sand alone would be brought in. It was expected that apart from sand, coal and other imports from the Bristol Channel would be carried to the interior and that granite and manganese would be able to be exported.

Despite the people who were against the canal, the committee were convinced that the canal would be worth all the work that would be put in. A survey of the parishes showed that 28,038 tons of sand were taken up annually.

This next cutting is taken from the Committee's report to the subscribers on 15th April 1818:

"By the present conveyance, the farmer, distant ten miles, can only go three times a week during the spring and summer months and, with three horses, draws only eight seams, or one ton, that distance in one day - by the improved plan, one horse will draw twenty tons the same distance so that three horses will bring sixty tons, and going at all seasons of the year will if employed every alternate day for the purpose, bring one hundred and twenty times as much as can be procured at present by the same number of horses."

The subscribers met again on 5th November, 1818, where various points were discussed. The following year Lord Stanhope approached the Duke of Bedford on the subject of repealing the Tamar Manure Navigation Act to enable the canal to be built to Launceston. The Duke was in favour of this because it would have avoided his estate at Endsleigh, but the plan did not take place, as an Act of Parliament was obtained in 1819.

And so the scene was set for the great undertaking to begin. At that time a big step forward in the history of this remote part of rural England.

Boating on the canal - a popular pastime then as now

CHAPTER TWO

The Construction of the Canal

The Bude Harbour and Canal Company was formed in the first half of 1819. There were 330 shareholders - leading subscribers were Earl and Countess Stanhope, Sir William and Lady Call, George Call (the company's first Chairman), Sir Arscott Molesworth, Sir Thomas Dyke Acland and William Arundel Harris. James Green, the appointed engineer, also invested a substantial sum. The Company was based in Exeter for the shareholders' convenience and also perhaps, because of the interests of the Acland's of Killerton, Exeter, who owned the Bude Harbour lands. Most of the company meetings were held at the New London Inn in the city.

The Act

On 14th June 1819 an Act was obtained "for improving the Harbour of Bude in the county of Cornwall, and for making and maintaining a navigable Canal from the said harbour of Bude, to or near the village of Thornbury, in the county of Devon and divers branches therefrom, all in the said counties of Cornwall and Devon."

A working ketch "Bude Packet" at the sea lock

Powers were given to raise £95,000 in 1,900 shares of £50 each and an additional sum of £20,000 if needed. Green's plan had been cut down to £91,617, which included £4,618 for harbour works. The Canal's eastward extension from Holsworthy across Dunsland Moor and towards Okehampton was scrapped and the terminus of the southern line was to be at Druxton, 3 miles short of the original point at Rushgrove Hill, Launceston. The Canal's north-easterly line was to end between Thornbury and Bradford, at Bason Lane, five miles from Holsworthy. Provision was made for a cut to Moreton Mill and to Langford Moor to act as a feeder from the reservoir (Tamar Lake) and for navigation to Virworthy, a distance of about 5 miles.

The length of 2 miles from Bude to Helebridge would be suitable for large barges and the rest of the canal for tub-boats. In all a total length of just under 46 miles.

The Beginning of Construction

No time was lost in starting the work of construction, which began on 23rd July 1819.

The day before, Lord Stanhope's carriage was drawn into Stratton by the local populace - bands played and "handsome entertainment" was provided. On the following morning, the ceremonies started early. Bells were rung - a "feu de joie" was fired. Lord Stanhope laid the first stone of the Breakwater and then cut the first sod of earth at the site of the Canal basin. Bands played 'God save the King' and 'Rule Britannia' and everyone returned to Summerleaze Down for further festivities - eating, drinking, dancing and wrestling.

Not enough suitable local labour was available to undertake the construction work and hundreds of navigators (navvies) were brought in to do the skilled work.

Throughout 1820 to 1822 many gangs worked on various parts of the canal simultaneously. For example, the Holsworthy line - the reservoir - the Breakwater - the aqueduct at Burmsden, and the locks and the Launceston line as far as Tamerton Bridge.

We can get an idea of the construction and progress on the canal by extracts from John Kingdon, the Company Inspector, in his diary. Another man, John Panchen, has written the majority of the earlier entries.

"Thursday, 19th October, 1820: In company with the Chairman walking to the Tunnel near Hammetts Lane and inspected the whole of the line of the canal from that point to Roydon Moor. Some few of the fences out of repair, but in general the whole was in good order. No workmen on this part of the line.

The Construction of the Canal

Friday 20th October, 1820: In company with the Chairman examined the whole of the line from Little Bridge to Red Post ... then took the eastern line from the branch bridge to Pancrasweek Valley ... then back to Burmsden and up the navigable feeder to the Reservoir on which branch found about sixty men at work. Inspected and found the culvert in good condition.

Saturday, 21st October 1820: ... examined line from Red Post to Bude, observed some leaks in the canal at Thurlibeer.

Sunday, 22nd October, 1820: Remained at Bude in company with the Chairman watching the effect of the high tide and seas on the Breakwater and Sea Lock. Counted on the work, 340 men.

Wednesday, 6th December, 1820: Placed twelve marks in the sand at Bude ... party of masons building a bridge near Hele Bridge where the course of the stream is finished. Parties at work on Abbacott (Hobbacott) and Marhamchurch Incline Planes and about 40 men excavating the sea lock channel.

Thursday, 14th December, 1820: The shaft at Marhamchurch Incline for the water wheel to work is fallen in. A gang of workmen dealing with it.

Wednesday, 27th December, 1820: One of the whims (a horse powered hoist for raising waste material) at Abbacott at work and one shaft expected to be clear of water this night. Plane partly formed and each shaft down about 70 feet and the adit driven about 60 feet.

Wednesday, 24th January, 1821: 25 men employed at the reservoir, some of whom are throwing back the bog and wallowing in rubbish ... nearly the

Tub-boats and the schooner "Infanta" - Capt. Pascoe; ketch Elizabeth - Capt. Lashbrook; and smack Mirre - Capt. Bate - May 1875. Note the little white gate marking the entrance to the Acland holiday cottages.

whole line from the reservoir to the Tamar is now open, but many parts in an unfinished state.

On the 5th March, 1821, water was let into the canal basin at high tide. On the 21st April, 1821 John Kingdon took a barge for a trial run, from the basin through the sea lock. He recorded in his diary:-

April 21st, 1821: Took the Barge No 1 out the sea lock and put on board her about 24 tons of sand, pm at tide time got her into the Basin, the Barge drawing 3ft 6in aft and 2ft 10in forward. Laid down the Buoys with mooring stones to place Barge on the sand. The easternmost Buoy 100 yards from the narrowest part of the channel.

April 25th, 1821: Towed the barge to Hele Bridge. Discharged the sand on the wharf and moored her.

June 26th, 1821: At the reservoir great leaks.

November 13th, 1821: From Burmsdon to the end of Lanson line now open. 13 masons finishing the bridge at Burmsdon, 5 men working on the quarry between Burmsdon and Anderton, no more from there to Red Post; the gangs on the Lanson line I could not count, the weather so bad they could not work.

December 22nd, 1821: Could not go on any part of the line owing to a fall from my horse."

Apparently, a lot of the Inspector's time was taken up in dealing with farmers' complaints over boundaries, fencing, damage to crops and livestock, either falling into the canal or straying.

Financial Difficulties

By 1821 doubts were raised concerning the profits to be made from the canal and the capital needed to complete it, although at the time, work was

The massive sea-lock with the iron bridge for the sand rails on Summerleaze beach.

The Construction of the Canal

progressing well. It was agreed to suspend the construction of the Thornbury line and to halt work on the Druxton line. Lord Stanhope proposed that sand should be transported from the beach to the basin by trucks on a railroad instead of by barge (at 1d per ton cheaper). Off-loading and re-loading at Hele Bridge was expensive and time-consuming.

On 8th July 1823, the official opening of the completed sections took place at Holsworthy. The committee of management supported by the "neighbouring gentry" marched into Holsworthy in procession, the band played "See The Conquering Hero Comes" (Mr Blackmore of Exeter, a Trader and Shareholder), and bells were rung from St Peter's Church. A dinner was provided at the Stanhope Arms (now Barclays Bank) where numerous toasts were drunk.

However, capital funds had run low and on 26th June, 1823 application was made to the Exchequer Bill Loan Commissioners for a loan of £20,000 - later reduced to £16,000.

This loan was approved and work on the southern route from Tamerton Bridge to Druxton began in 1824, by which time there were already 100 boats operating on the canal. A further £4,000 was still needed and another loan from the commissioners was obtained.

Work was finally completed in 1825 with the total cost of constructing the canal amounting to just under £120,000.

A lovely shot of the schooner Brackley - Capt. Hollingsworth and the ketch Margaret - Capt. Rees in the lower basin.

CHAPTER THREE

The Route of the Canal and its Unique Features

An important and vital feature of the whole undertaking was the Breakwater at Bude. Built from the mainland to Chapple (now Chapel) rock, with a bango-type granite pierhead beyond, it protected the great sea-lock and also shipping in the haven.

It was a truly massive structure faced with granite and limestone, but internally composed of clay and rubble, 900ft long, about 20ft high with an upper width of 10ft. A terrible storm in February 1838 virtually destroyed this Breakwater and after a petition by six Bude sea-captains, was rebuilt to a different design the following year. Replacement stone was brought by sea from the Vale of Lanherne near Newquay to Bude and also by a small light railway from the other side of Compass Point (metal fixings can still be seen on the rocks beyond Whale rock).

The river Strat (now Neet) that ran under Summerleaze was diverted to its present southerly route and deepened to allow vessels to enter the Haven around high-water.

The massive sea-lock, after reconstruction in 1835 measured 116' x 29' 6" with a depth of water of 9' 6" at the cill. This lock allowed ships of 300 tons to enter the basin where the depth of water was 10ft. Beside the northern arm of the lock is a 2ft tramway, originally 4ft, on which horses pulled end-tipping sand trucks from the beach to the waiting tub-boats at the "sand wharf". (A turntable can still be seen just beyond the iron bridge.)

Past the blacksmith's forge (now the Town Museum) was the "Company Wharf", on the lower basin, later to become Hockin's timber yard and Petherick's coal store.

The Falcon swing-bridge (now solid) allowed vessels into Sir Thomas Acland's private wharf on the right-hand side of the upper basin. The lifeboat also used the canal, the swingbridge and

Rodd's Bridge lock in its operational days

The Route of the Canal and its Unique Features

sea-lock at high-water. The tub-boats, measuring 20' x 5' 6" x 1' 8" with a capacity of 4 - 5 tons, continued inland past a lay-bye to the first lock at Rodd's Bridge, length 63ft, width 14' 7", rise 5' 6" and on to Helebridge wharf through the second lock at Whalesborough with the same measurements. For the first 1¾ miles the depth of water in the canal was 4' 6", afterwards only 3ft deep and 10ft wide at the bottom (hardly enough for commercial and pleasure craft today).

The wooden tub-boats originally had four small wheels of 14" diameter protruding outside the sides of the boat to run in the channel rails on the inclined planes, but because of damage to the canal banks on corners and in high cross-winds, these wheels were placed in slots built internally under the sides of the boat. The train of boats at first consisted of six boats, which was found to be unmanageable and reduced to four. They were steered by a boatman with a handspike standing in the second boat, or from the bank and only the leading boat had a pointed bow. The large barges - 50' x 13' x 3' 6" capacity 20 tons were soon abandoned because of the extra work in loading, unloading and reloading at Helebridge.

How did the Inclined Planes work?

The following description of the workings of inclined planes by a Mr Venning of Marhamchurch is taken from "A Map for Ramblers" published

The famous canal aqueduct over the river Tamar taking the canal into Devon

by Arthur A. Isaac, Bude, in the late twenties. If only actual plans/drawings/designs were available, it would do much to solve the mystery of how the machinery worked, but these extracts go a long way in our understanding of the operation of supplying power to raise or lower the tub-boats.

The first of six inclined planes to be reached was at Marhamchurch, 2 miles from the sea-lock. This plane raised the level a further 120ft in a distance of 836ft. Motive power was provided by a 50′ diameter, 3ft wide overshot waterwheel which operated an enormous endless chain over a winding drum to draw the boats up one or two at a time. At the top and also at the bottom of the plane were two great chain wheels, mounted at right angles to the angle of the plane on heavy baulks of timber forming a frame with the great chain wheels overhead. The wheels were grooved around the periphery to carry the heavy chain that propelled the boats up and down the plane, the diameter of the wheels being great enough to allow the chains to run in the centre of the tracks on which the boats travelled. There were two 24 inch "jockey" pulleys with similarly grooved rims to take the weight of the sagging chains as they approached and left the great wheels and fell on the sleeves or rollers in the centre of each track. There were semaphores at top and bottom of the plane for signalling purposes. At the bottom and top of the plane were narrow channels on each side just wide enough for one boat to float, with a central stone pier. Standing on the centre pier was a man with a boat hook who guided the boat under the great chain, which fell into an iron-bound "V" groove fitted in the bow to receive it. As soon as the chain caught in the front "V" the boat was propelled up the incline on to the rails of the plane and the chain lay along the centre of the boat, catching another of its links in the "V" at the stern of the boat. The links of this enormous endless chain were composed of 1 inch solid iron and the barges travelled up one side full and down the other side empty.

Barges could be pulled up one or two at a time and if empty, two or three could descend at a time. On a boat reaching the top, its wheels left the rails and it glided away in the narrow channel into the wider canal.

Sometimes the chain would stick in the front groove and the boat front would be carried up towards the "jockey" pulley, before falling with a splash into the canal. The overshot water wheel was of the bucket type, with a leat feed from the upper canal; its two enormous gear wheels, one on the water wheel shaft, and the other above and geared with it, drove a horizontal shaft at the top of the pit, through a pinion on the end of this shaft. This horizontal shaft drove the nearly vertical chain wheel through a pair of bevel gears. A sluice and leat also supplied water to a small waterwheel at Box's Iron Foundry.

The Route of the Canal and its Unique Features

The route passed immediately north of Marhamchurch village, through Cann Orchard, to Hobbacott Down to the largest incline in the system. Rising 225ft, 935ft in length, Hobbacott plane, like the others, was worked by waterpower. Here the system consisted of two wells sunk at the top of the plane, in each of which the descent of a bucket, 9' in diameter, 5' 6" deep, suspended on a double chain wound over a geared drum and containing 15 tons of water.

The buckets were in counterpoise and the weight of water as the bucket at the top filled caused the empty bucket to ascend to the surface while the full bucket sank down its shaft, turning gearing, shafting, chain wheels and chain in a very similar manner to that on the Marhamchurch Plane. When the full bucket reached the bottom of the shaft a valve was automatically opened and the bucket emptied, the other bucket at the top was filled and the process was repeated until the chain had completed its circuit; each bucket making two journeys up and down in order to revolve the great chain once.

This system provided the power for raising the loaded boats. As a standby, a 16ft steam engine was also kept at the top of the plane and brought into use when the endless chains broke, which they did frequently.

There was also a small waterwheel of 9ft diameter to provide power to the Canal's blacksmith's shop at Hobbacott.

Box's iron foundry, Marhamchurch. Note the waterwheel in the centre of the large building

The canal then ran eastwards to Red Post, where there was a wharf just before passing under the Kilkhampton-Launceston road (B3254) and shortly afterwards divided into it's two main branches. The main trunk route to Holsworthy then took a wide sweep around Shernick - passed under the Holsworthy - Bude road (A3072) - around Anderton to Burmsdon. At this point the canal crossed the river Tamar by a fine stone single-arched aqueduct, entered Devon and approached the next inclined plane known as Vealand, Veala or Venn. A waterwheel raised the canal a further 58' in a distance of 500' taking it to the summit level of about 423ft (129m).

At Brendon Moor, the main canal to Holsworthy turned right at the junction with the feeder canal, it continued over a large embankment at Thorn Farm, across fields to Canal Farm at Chilsworthy, crossing the river Deer by a large aqueduct before winding its way to Stanbury Wharf and Blagdon Moor wharf, both with store houses and a wharfinger's house. This was the end of the Holsworthy line.

The feeder branch passed under eleven bridges to reach Virworthy Mill Wharf and Virworthy Wharf and basin. This was the terminus for tub-boats, but water was fed from the 70 acre reservoir made by erecting an embankment or dam across the river Tamar, which was also fed by several small streams. The lake held 195 million gallons with an average depth of 12 feet, and provided water for the whole tub-boat system.

The Launceston branch started at Red Post near the main road (A3072) and continued south keeping to the west of the river Tamar for the whole way. The first wharf was at Littlebridge, Bridgerule, just west of the village. The first of the branches three waterwheel-worked descending incline planes was at Merrifield, which had a fall of 60ft and a length of 360ft. At North Tamerton there were two wharves, one for coal and the other for sand. Store houses and wharfinger's house straddle the road where the canal was taken across on a low aqueduct.

A mile further on was the Tamerton inclined plane also 36ft long and with a descent of 59ft. There was a wharf and basin with the usual buildings (no longer visible) at Boyton.

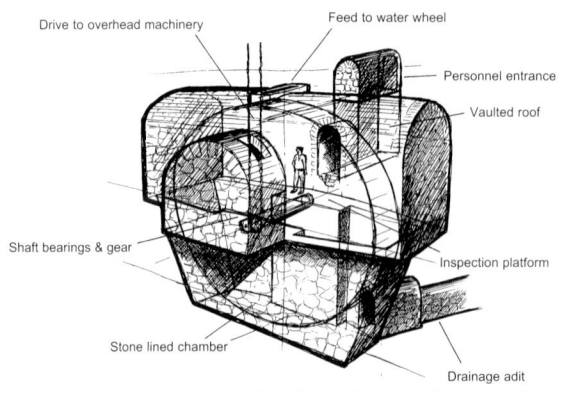

A cutaway drawing showing the workings of an undergeround waterwheel pit

The Route of the Canal and its Unique Features

The canal continued under Haunch Bridge, across an aqueduct at Tamertown, to the Werrington plane, which had a fall of 51ft and in its length of 259ft passed over the slightly lowered road by means of a stone arch.

Another aqueduct allowed it to cross Tala water before reaching its southern terminus at Druxton Wharf (Crossgate), 3 miles short of Launceston. At Crossgate, there were the usual store houses, stables and a Wharfinger's house.

Besides the well-built aqueducts and underground waterwheel pits, there were numerous farm and "accommodation" bridges, and solid stone-faced culverts that carried leats for mills, or streams to the river Tamar. The substantial stone bridges over the canal were built to a standard design, and the best examples (that still stand today) are at Helebridge, Burmsdon, Thorne Farm and Haunch Bridge at Boyton.

The whole system was well-planned and exceedingly ingenious, and when in order, worked well.

Unfortunately, the actual construction and the materials used resulted in frequent breakdowns, particularly on the inclined planes. Loss of trade and the cost of repairs far exceeded the original estimations.

The sand wharf with tub boats being loaded with sand from the side-tipping trucks

CHAPTER FOUR

The Canal's Decline and Demise

Following the boom years of the early 1840's the canal worked its way through the 1850's and into the 1860's with a general decline in takings - partly due to improvements in road transport and also the actual effects of railway development in the West Country. However, the structural expenditure was less and the debt to the Exchequer Bill Loan Commissioners had been finally paid off; 1859 was the year that showed the highest profit of £1,493.

The Effect of the Railways

When the Bude Canal was opened in 1823 the "railways" had hardly existed, but by the 1870's their national network was widespread, offering cheap transport for both passengers and freight in direct competition with the country's canal systems.

For example, there had been the possibility of severe railway competition when a Parliamentary Act dated 28th July 1836 was obtained for making and maintaining a harbour, breakwater and a lighthouse at Tremoutha Haven in the manor of Crackington at St Gennys, with a new town there to be called Victoria and a railway connecting it to Launceston, but fortunately for the Bude canal, the plan never materialised.

However, Exeter had been reached from London via Bristol in 1844 and Penzance in 1852. In 1864 the Launceston and South Devon Railway opened connecting Launceston with Tavistock and Plymouth.

In the next year, there was even an attempt to construct a railway, $2^1/_2$ miles long, to connect the Bude canal basin at Druxton with the Launceston Junction Railway Company, with a capital of £20,000.

The aim being to take the Bude sand even further inland. This scheme did not materialise however. In efforts to compete with the railway, tolls on sand and other goods were lowered, causing a temporary increase in the tonnage of sand carried, but bringing in less money.

Early in 1879, the London and South Western Railway reached Holsworthy (only 10 miles from Bude) by a branch line from Meldon near Okehampton. Ironically, the extensive festivities at Holsworthy were lead by Lord and Lady Stanhope, who were direct descendants of the Lord Stanhope who had started the construction of the Bude Canal with such enthusiasm 60 years before in 1819.

The Canal's Decline and Demise

At first the sale of sand went up dramatically as the sand was taken further inland by rail. In fact, at Stanbury Wharf, which had a good stock of coal and sand, trade was particularly brisk.

Holsworthy served as a railhead for Bude for nearly twenty years until on 10th August 1898 the railway finally reached Bude via Whitstone and Bridgerule station.

However, farmers were now turning to the artificial fertilisers and lime from other sources. And from then on, there was also a swift drop in the tonnage of coal carried by the waterway and harbour and basin dues at Bude also showed a similar downward trend. Nevertheless, it was in these later and declining years that the Company's only dividends were paid. The first came in 1876, six years after the debt to the Exchequer Bill Loan Commissioners had been paid off and fifty three years after the canal opened. This amounted to 10s per £50 share. The last dividend of 2/6d per share was paid in 1899.

Repair and Maintenance

Despite everything, maintenance of the works throughout the whole system continued to be carried out in a very satisfactory manner, well into

Helebridge basin and inclined plane showing abandoned tub boats, C 1900

the 1880's. Mr George Casebourne, the resident engineer for 40 years, died in 1876 and Nicholas Sullivan of Exeter was appointed in his place. He was an excellent engineer and was constantly praised by the Committee for "much improving" the general state of the canal and works. Even so, the steam engine and boiler at Hobbacott had become worn out and were sold. Wages and salaries were reduced and where possible, consistent with safety, men were sacked.

The Beginning of the End

In February 1884 Vivian's, one of the main merchants, announced that they would not be trading any more. The Management Committee prepared a report that in effect stated that there was no future for the canal and recommended that an Act of Abandonment be applied for from Parliament.

A special Assembly of Proprietors was called to recommend this, but on 30th January 1885 not enough people were present and the canal stayed open. Vivian's continued trading for a short time.

The Committee withdrew the Abandonment Act of 1884, but the ultimate decline of the canal came a step nearer with the passing of the "Bude Harbour and Canal (Further Powers) Act on 3rd July 1891, which authorised abandonment of the branches from Red Post to Druxton and from Brendon Moor Junction to Blagdonmoor, but retaining portions of the canal and in particular, the harbour, the barge canal, the aqueduct and the reservoir (Tamar Lake).

The final acts of the Bude Canal as a full trading enterprise were now slowly being played out.

The inclined plane at Werrington passing over the Bridgetown road

The ketch "Annie Davey" locking-in

The Bude Canal: Past & Present

A peaceful summer scene on the barge canal at Rodd's Bridge

Chilsworthy embankment taking the canal over the river Deer

Lower Tamar Lake - the reservoir for the canal system - now a nature reserve

The bottom of Hobbacott inclined plane showing adits and boat bays

The original breakwater, destroyed in 1838 by a great storm.

The swing bridge between the Upper and Lower Basins of Bude Wharf before being replaced by the current fixed bridge.

A 50' barge, loaded with sand being locked in at Rodd's Bridge, one mile inland. The sand would be transferred into the tub-boats at Helebridge Wharf.

36

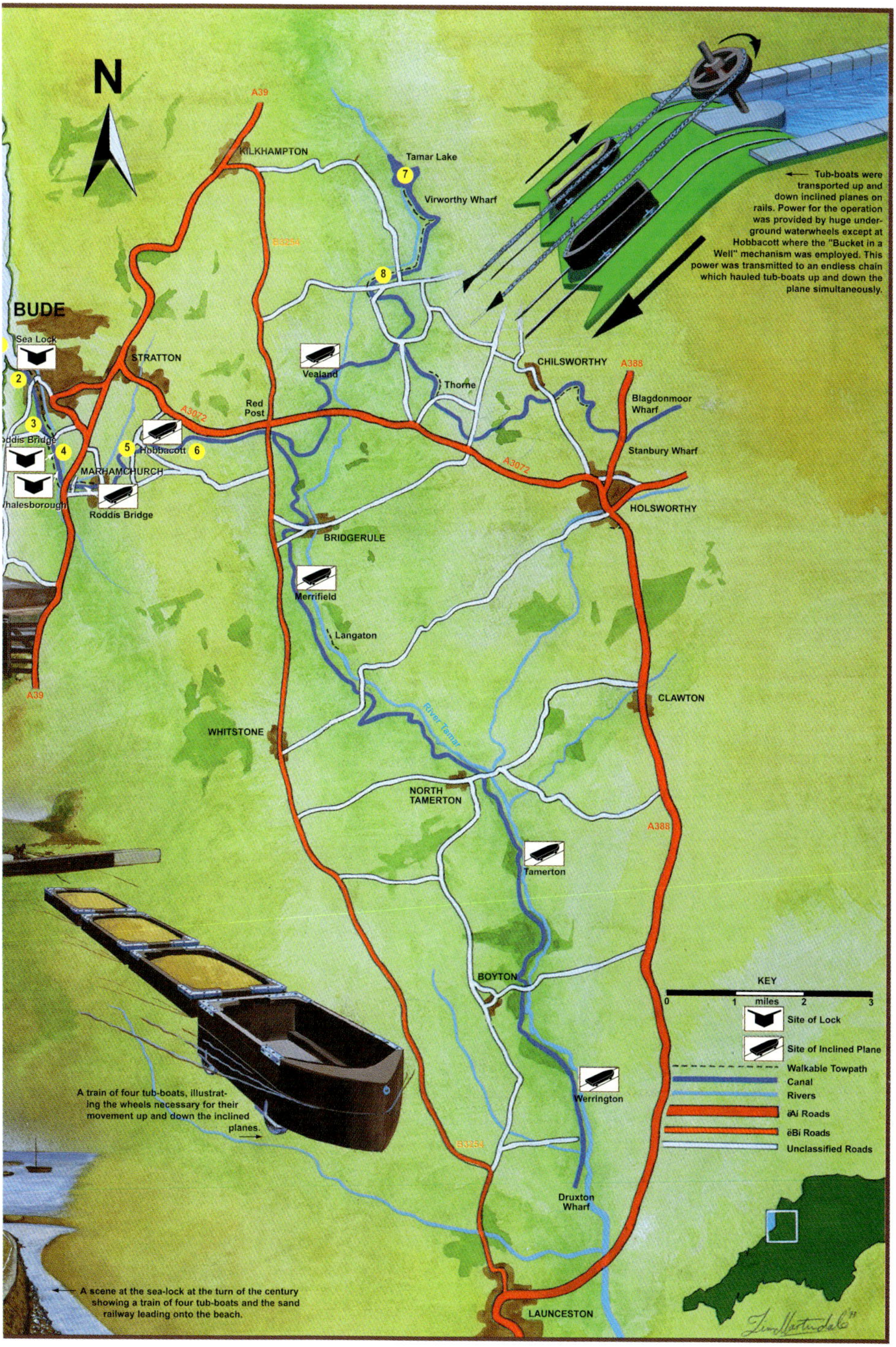
N
A39
KILKHAMPTON
Tamar Lake
Virworthy Wharf
B3254
BUDE
Sea Lock
STRATTON
Vealand
Thorne
CHILSWORTHY
A388
Blagdonmoor Wharf
Red Post
A3072
Hobbacott
MARHAMCHURCH
Roddis Bridge
Whalesborough
Stanbury Wharf
HOLSWORTHY
BRIDGERULE
Merrifield
Langaton
CLAWTON
WHITSTONE
River Tamar
NORTH TAMERTON
Tamerton
BOYTON
Werrington
Druxton Wharf
LAUNCESTON
Tub-boats were transported up and down inclined planes on rails. Power for the operation was provided by huge underground waterwheels except at Hobbacott where the "Bucket in a Well" mechanism was employed. This power was transmitted to an endless chain which hauled tub-boats up and down the plane simultaneously.
A train of four tub-boats, illustrating the wheels necessary for their movement up and down the inclined planes.
A scene at the sea-lock at the turn of the century showing a train of four tub-boats and the sand railway leading onto the beach.
KEY
0 1 miles 2 3
Site of Lock
Site of Inclined Plane
Walkable Towpath
Canal
Rivers
'A' Roads
'B' Roads
Unclassified Roads

The Bude Canal: Past & Present

The towpath and basin at Helebridge

The canal at Helebridge

CHAPTER FIVE

The Passing of a Great Engineering Enterprise, and the Creation of a Water Supply for Stratton and Bude

Way back in 1886 there were various recommendations for increasing income; by raising charges to firms renting the Wharves at Bude for timber, by increasing rates payable by various concerns (including Box's foundry at Marhamchurch) for use of water, and by raising the charge for fishing in the reservoir - then let to the Rev. WH Montgomery for trout breeding and shooting rights - from £3 10s 0d. to £5 a year.

The Company charged 21s each a year for pleasure boats on the canal, while small sums were also raised from the letting of withy beds on the canal route.

The arrival of piped water in Bude - opened by General Redfern Buller in 1903

In spite of all the problems, right up to 1890, maintenance works and repairs were diligently attended to - making up the towing paths; repairing culverts, renewing clay puddling, ditching, fencing and the planting of withies, repairing the inclined planes, and finally, repairs to the sea-lock.

In 1887 the Falcon bridge was widened at the request of the National Lifeboat Institution.

When the long delayed construction of the Holsworthy-Bude railway finally started in 1896 the Canal Company asked the London and South Western Railway to buy them out, but it was too late and they declined. Surprisingly, there was still a steady flow of trade into the port of Bude itself, and some of the railway construction materials, sleepers, etc., having been brought in by sea were even taken inland by canal.

At this time it was realised that the reservoir at Tamar lake would be a superb water supply for the now growing seaside resort of Bude:

The "Gem of the West" as a current poem had it.

Protracted negotiations began with the Stratton Rural Sanitary Authority, but instead they wanted to make a reservoir at Halls, north of Stratton. In fact, they did not get the loan required to carry out the scheme and the idea was dropped.

The Act of 1891, besides authorising the abandonment of the two main branches of the canal, also made provision for a regular and continuous flow of water from the reservoir along the canal to the top of the Hobbacott plane, for which the local authority was to pay the Canal Company 1d per 1000 gallons up to 60,000 gallons a day and ½d per 1000 gallons in excess; the local authority to construct and maintain the necessary sluices, filter beds and piping. The Act also sanctioned an arrangement which had been made by Edward Mucklow JP of Whitstone for the supply of water from the Canal Company for property belonging to him in the parishes of Marhamchurch and Poundstock. ("Mucklow was a wealthy Lancashire chemical manufacturer who had purchased the Whitstone Estate in 1875".) It soon became apparent that the supply of water taken from the open canal at Hobbacott would be scarcely fit for domestic purposes. This unsatisfactory and unresolved situation dragged on through 1893 and 1894.

After enquiries from the newly formed Stratton Rural District Council, the Committee recommended acceptance by the shareholders of the sum of £8000 for the whole of the assets. In 1900, however, further negotiations proceeded between the Stratton and Bude Urban District Council, and the company. The Council resolved to promote a Bill to Parliament for the purpose of purchasing the entire undertaking at the previously agreed figure.

These discussions resulted in the "Stratton and Bude Improvement Act", being passed by Parliament and given the royal assent on 17th April 1901.

The Passing of a Great Engineering Enterprise, and the Creation of a Water Supply

Sold for one-fifteenth of its original cost, the Canal was formally handed over to the Council on 1st January 1902, and two months later sums amounting to £4 per share were paid out to the various shareholders. The Bude Canal as an inland waterway had reached its eventual, but inevitable demise.

Soon after acquiring ownership of the Canal's remaining length, including the Barge canal, the Harbour basin and the Breakwater, but minus the Holsworthy and Launceston branches, the Stratton and Bude Urban District Council began construction of its new waterworks. The existing 4¾ mile stretch of canal leading from the reservoir was retained as an open aqueduct and the water extracted at Venn. Here, near the top of the Vealand plane, filter beds were made as authorised by the Act of 1901, and piping was laid to carry the water after treatment to the Urban area.

General Redvers Buller of Boer War fame opened the whole water supply proceedings with great aplomb from a grandstand in the centre of Bude on Saturday, 23rd May 1903. Here, under a mighty banner proclaiming - "Success to our West Country Health Resort" the General made his speech -

"I can assure you it is for many reasons a very great pleasure to me to make my first visit to this beautiful place (hear, hear!) upon an occasion so interesting and so advantageous to its welfare" (hear, hear!) etc., etc.

The lay-by in the upper basin with abandoned tub boats and the new railway siding to the lower wharf C1900

41

As a memento the General was presented with an inscribed silver cup. The whole event was followed by a large lunch in the Parish Hall with the Town Band playing outside. In the afternoon the same procedure was followed in Stratton. This surely was a fitting finale to this part of the Canal's final curtain call.

The cathedral-like undergound waterwheel pit at North Tamerton

CHAPTER SIX
Life on the Canal Part I

In the preceding chapters the simple history of the canal has been given in some detail, but facts alone do not give the whole picture, particularly, for example, where people worked, how they worked and who they were. Naturally enough on this part of the coast, extremes of weather occasionally affected the working of the canal. When there was drought and the reservoir dropped below working level, and the need to allow sufficient water to pass for mills downstream, the canal had to be temporarily closed; it was also generally closed when harvesting was in progress and "moonlighting" was not unknown. For example, the wife of the wharfinger at North Tamerton, Mrs Smale, was given a bell by the Company to summon her husband from nearby fields when a train of boats appeared. Icing over in severe weather was also a problem, and two horses were used to pull a boat at 4 m.p.h. to clear a passage.

The "Alford" passing through the iron swing bridge to reach the upper basin

John Honey and his letters

John Honey had been appointed clerk to the Company at Bude in 1824 and remained in the Company's employment until 1832. During these years, he moved into a house at Hobbacott Down, at the top of the plane, succeeding a Mr Whitewood. He was well liked by many people in the district, including George Call, who backed him on many occasions, particularly concerning his monthly reports to the Committee of Management. His diary and reports make very interesting reading. At times he seems to have shouldered many of the engineering responsibilities in addition to his clerical work. In 1826 Mr Call wrote "I agree with him on all points particularly on the necessity of repairing the railways on the Planes". In 1827 he wrote "The last month has been a period of misfortune and they have followed each other so quickly that Mr Honey and his assistant have had the most severe duty to perform. I leave you gentlemen to judge of the exertion of the former when I state that he rode three hundred miles in five days and I am astonished at his having been able to stand up against such fatigue. I trust gentlemen that you will allow me to suggest the propriety of noting his good conduct in your Resolutions".

Nevertheless, there were those who failed to appreciate the difficulties of the situation and did not always give the men on the spot the support they deserved. Life for Mr Honey meant coping with the frequent breakdowns, accidents and damage which occurred and trying to find sufficient money for paying taxes, to pay tradespeople for materials and spare parts supplied, labourers for their wages and various individuals for occasional incidental damages.

From a series of lengthy letters written by John Honey between 29th October 1830 and 27th March 1832 to Mr J Blackmore and J W Crabb, both of Exeter and chairmen in turn of the Committee of Management, and to others including T Shearm, the company's land surveyor, it is possible to form a picture of events. There were difficulties in getting answers and decisions, and delays over repairs while these were awaited and until overdue parts were received. These extracts will give you some idea of the problems with which Mr Honey had to contend:-

23 December 1830 'I beg further to inform you that the connecting shafts between the waterwheel and the Chain Wheel shaft at Tamerton Town plane broke on Tuesday last in taking up some returning boats over the Plane, I went on yesterday with Geake and investigated the particulars and I am making a Model for a Cast Iron Clip to mend the shaft, and hope to get it cast tomorrow & fixed up on Monday next, when it will be in proper order for the Trade again if there should be any'.

Life on the Canal Part I

9 January 1831 'I informed the Committee when at Exeter that the Wheels at Tamerton, Merrifield & Bridgetown Inclined planes wanted new hanging. The men (mechanics) of these planes being all discharged I cannot do it, therefore I hope you will attach no blame to me in case of accidents when the work should again recommence; I also informed the Committee that a quantity of fences throughout the line was necessary to be done, having only 5 labourers in $35^{1}/_{2}$ miles of Canal this cannot be attended to all throughout, great trespass of cattle will be the result'.

11 February 1831 'I am extremely sorry to inform you that the Boiler of the steam engine is rusted through in many places, which prevents us from working at present in any way at this place (Hobbacott Down).'

6 April 18431 'I have examined and repaired Marhamchurch Machinery so far as I can (viz) in putting all the Gear to run correctly, and have put new bearing Brasses under the Water Wheel shaft and rose it up to its correct level and height. This shaft had worn through the bearing Brasses and working on the cast iron carriage, which was highly improper ... The wood framing is in many places extremely rotten, something must be done to it soon, otherwise the iron machinery which is at present supported by it, must be damaged considerably.'

Shipping in Bude at its hey-day 1897. See page 72 for names and masters

'I have thoroughly examined the state of the machinery of all the small Inclined Planes as to the Gear, the manner in which it now runs and also the wood framing that supports it; there is much wanted and actually necessary to be done, both, as to fixing the Gear more correctly & supplying new framing in a great many places where the old is rotten and defective.'

I am repairing the Steam Boiler and shall lose no time in putting it in proper repair.'

... Your late engineer has actually built cob (or mud walls) on each side of the valleys next the water, for the purpose of strengthening them. The poor labour men who were obliged to do it under his instructions told him that they knew too well the nature of cob walls (from their own cottages) for it to answer any purpose wherein it was kept in the least degree wet, much more so, where it was always under water his answer was to them (as in all cases) let it be right or wrong do as I tell you, then you'll have no fault, and when they would say they thought it would not answer, he would say in answer

d--n thee, thee has no right to think, I must think for I am paid for thinking, and thee for working, therefore do as I tell thee or be off.'

28 June 1831 'It is necessary the Steam Engine be immediately put in repair, in case an accident should happen at Hobbacott Down to the Bucket Machinery.'

13 August 1831 'About half past twelve o'clock this day a man named John Wilkey a boatman in Mr King's employ in the act of taking down some empty boats from the Top of Hobbacott Plane, hooked on three nos 30, 45 & 46 and put the shackle on the Main Chain in the regular way; immediately as the two foremost boats came out over the Top of the Plane, this man Wilkey who was in the foremost boat was seen by Wm Dyer a mason working for the Company removing or handling the Shackle; and by this means the Boats escaped from their fastening & run from Top to bottom of the Plane; on examining the foremost boat, I found the V which the Main Chain falls into also broken as they came to the bottom the foremost boat ran immediately into the centre of the Work and Broke the shaft of the Chain Wheel and several of the Wood arms & has considerably damaged the framing. This accident and damage has been occasioned through the mismanagement of the Boatmen.'

23 November 1830 'It being now Market Day at Stratton where the Mechanics & Labourers get their supply for the ensuing week I have had almost the whole of them ... requesting to be paid their wages, as otherwise they inform me they cannot procure necessaries for their support ... Messrs H & J James have applied to me for payment of the amount due to them for Sundry Goods ... I have been called on this morning by no less than 10 persons for Taxes. I've not a farthing to pay them, and worse than all this

there is no Trade whatsoever on the Canal and only 177 Boats have been taken over the Planes from the 1st of this month to the present time. This Trade will not pay for Coals and Labour in passing the different planes... The farmers are going to the Beach for sand & to the Lime Kilns for Lime ...'

16 December 1830 'If there is no trade there can be no income, and I cannot compel the Traders to work. I've done all I can both with the Traders and farmers and the former informs me they cannot sell their sand if they take it up, if there are to pay the Tolls now demanded, the latter informs me they cannot purchase sand at the price the Traders sell for, ... I am confident in my opinion that unless some alteration takes place immediately on the Tolls that the Company will have no money to pay the Taxes on the Canal.'

It is no wonder that John Honey felt tired and very frustrated. Yet even when he wrote to the Chairman, "I have walked myself until I am almost tired in that degree that I can scarcely walk any more", the committee still would not provide him with a horse, and when he himself borrowed one, it would not pay for a saddle and bridle! In 1832 he was given notice to quit and obviously felt resentment at his summary dismissal. He was succeeded by one of the James Green's assistants, Joseph Cox, who was then followed in 1834 by James Collom.

A 1930's summer scene watching the ketch "Ceres" entering the lower basin from the sea-lock

CHAPTER SEVEN

Life on the Canal Part II

Traders, Engineers and Employees

Four companies were trading on the canal in 1838 - H King, S Bray, H Rundle and B Adams. Each had to pay a certain sum of money to the company as security. Early in 1832 Rundle sold his boats to King and went to America and in 1841 Captain King RN, himself left the country on being appointed Chief Commissioner to the New Zealand Company, which prompted the Committee of Management to send him an address, noting "the honourable zeal" with which he had "so ably conducted the principal mercantile establishment of the Bude Canal". Capt. King accepted an offer by the company of £150 for the sale of a cottage at Druxton Wharf, coal sheds and stables at Stanbury Cross and Blagdonmoor, which the company subsequently let to Ham & Co.

By 1840, the Canal Company improved facilities at the wharves with the addition of coal yards and buildings; individual traders had their own allotments of space at the wharves, identified by their initials on iron stakes. In 1841 the firms of John Somers James and Co. and the Bude Canal Trading Company were operating on the Canal.

The men who worked on the canal, mechanics and labourers, where also praised by George Call the Company Chairman, when in the early period they had at times worked day and night on repairs. Nineteen men were employed in 1830, consisting of a lock-keeper, wharfingers, mechanics and others on the planes, masons and men who maintained the banks and fences. The company occasionally bestowed merits; in 1839 it resolves "That Thomas Smale employed at Tamerton be paid 2s instead of 1s 8d per day as a reward for his attentive conduct to his section of the line being in a better state than any others and being strongly recommended by the Engineer."

And in 1841 "that the sum of ten shillings be paid to the labourer whose portion of canal shall at the expiration of one year appear to Mr Vowler to be in the best order.

Engineers - James Green (1781 - 1849)

Probably because of his contacts in Exeter, as well as his reputation and the experience that he gained there, he was appointed the first engineer to the

Life on the Canal Part II

Bude Canal. He was an energetic man of far-seeing mind, usually self-confident and at times opinionated.

He was born in Birmingham in 1781, the son of an engineer with whom he worked until 1801, after which he was employed under John Rennie (1761 - 1821), the famous Bridge builder on various engineering projects throughout the country. Green was appointed Bridge Surveyor for the County of Devon, and in 1818 was made Surveyor of Bridges and Buildings for the county, a post which he held until 1841. At that time it was customary for county surveyors also to undertake private work. In 1810 Green prepared a plan for Lord Rolle for a Torridge canal from Torrington along the eastern side of the river past Weare Gifford to enter it just above Hallsfield opposite Landcross, just south of Bideford, but it all came to nothing. In 1818 James Green was asked to improve the Exeter Canal and in 1820 was commissioned to dredge and straighten the canal and to repair the double locks.

For years there had been an idea of a Canal linking both the Bristol and English Channels, thus saving ships the journey round Lands End. Several schemes had been proposed including one from the river Parrett to Seaton in South Devon via Chard in Somerset.

In 1821 (nearing the end of the construction of the Bude Canal) Green

Another summer Sunday outing

surveyed a line from the River Tones, and from the Bristol and Taunton canal, to Beer.

In 1823 he was called to report on the possibilities of a canal, a railway or a turnpike road between East and West Looe and Liskeard. He recommended incline planes and boats with a capacity of 4 tons (similar to the Bude Canal) but his advice was not accepted by the local committee.

In 1826 James Green was employed to consider the approach to Newton Abbott from Teignmouth. He proposed a canal a mile long with a tide lock at its entrance, running across shallows to a basin in the centre of the town. No action followed.

In 1829 - 1830 he was brought in to advise and report, with costings on the construction of the Grand Western Canal (Taunton to Tiverton) which also included an incline plane as well as lifts which he designed. The opening of the canal was delayed and he was blamed as the lifts were never given a fair trial. Practical difficulties developed in spite of his experience with the Bude and Torrington Canals. The Wellisford plane, 3 miles NW of Wellington, was built similar to Hobbacott Plane with two buckets in a well, but the buckets only carried 10 tons of water for 8 ton boats, whereas Hobbacott's buckets carried 15 tons of water for 4 ton boats. In 1836 Green ceased to be its engineer. Earlier in 1832 he had ceased to be the engineer for the Bude Canal. It's amazing how he found the time to dabble in all these projects and how he lasted so long with such divided loyalties.

George Casebourne was the Bude Canal engineer from 1832 - 1876 and for him home was a rather fine house beside the wharf at Helebridge, Marhamchurch. He was provided with a boat in which to patrol the canal and also a reserved mooring for it. He was a loyal and respected servant of the company until his death in 1876. His widow was given a gift of £50 in recognition of her husband's services. After Mr Casebourne's death, Nicholas Sullivan of Exeter was appointed Canal Engineer at a slightly increased salary of £12 10s 0d a month. He served until 1894 but was retained as "Consulting Engineer" until 1901.

George Casebourne, the able engineer who took over from James Green in 1832

Company Employees

Charles Brown worked at Hobbacott as conduitor for 3s 6d a day and was provided with a cottage. His assistant, Thomas Shepheard received 3s a day

Life on the Canal Part II

and also had a cottage. George Bond, a wharfinger at Hele Bridge, had only 2s 3d a day as did the mason William Dyer, described as "a man of much skill". In 1837 Thomas Brown Jnr, the canal carpenter, was paid 1s a day, but in 1878 James Sleeman, the then carpenter, had a craftsman's wage of 19s a week. In 1882 he was appointed planekeeper at Hobbacott, taking over the cottage formerly occupied by Charles Brown, who retired. Samuel Parnell of North Tamerton started work when Tamerton Wharf was built, he lived in the wharf cottage, one of a cluster of three dwellings alongside the aqueduct which was built to take the canal over the Holsworthy road. He started as boatman and his grave can be clearly identified in Tamerton churchyard.

John Gliddon started work on the canal as a boy leading the horses, at a wage of 2s 6d per week. He was a hard working, meticulous man who liked everything to run with almost military precision. He worked his way up to wharfinger at Blagdon Moor where he was known for his strict marshalling of the traffic there. He served at Holsworthy for ten years 1856 - 1866 and died at the age of 73. His grave is in Pancrasweek churchyard. His place at the wharf was taken by John Hutching.

Thomas Smale in 1839 was in charge of the Tamerton line and moved into a company cottage at the top of Tamerton Plane as planekeeper. An isolated and lonely post, but in 1843 he was promoted to a better house and more

The ketch "Ceres" unloading outside Pethericks coal yard - note Southern Railway truck on the siding

accessible location at Werrington plane. Thomas was buried on 29th April 1849 at the age of 56 in Werrington churchyard. John Smale followed as planekeeper at Werrington in 1871 and the third in line, Noah Smale, continued in 1891 until the canal closed but was allowed to remain living in the planekeeper's house after the closure. In 1899 he also died aged 56 and is also buried in Werrington churchyard.

The wharfingers at Druxton Wharf (Crossgate) were George Northey 1859 - John Crocker 1861 - William Sobey 1865 and finally Walter Smith. His son, also called Walter, helped his father at the wharf and died in 1859 aged 81.

In spite of poor pay, many hardships and long hours the whole work force from the engineers, clerks and labourers down to the boys leading the horses appear to have been loyal, hardworking and conscientious.

For 70 years they kept this unique Cornish Engineering Enterprise, the Bude Canal, in operation despite all the odds and indifferent management, a surely remarkable feat by superb craftsmen.

The lower basin showing tub boats and the ketch "Annie Davey" alongside Hockins timber yard

The Hobbacott plane buildings - John Honey's house and store house

CHAPTER EIGHT
The Twilight Years

For many years the length of the canal from Vealand, in Pancrasweek, to Helebridge lay idle and virtually untouched, yearly becoming more derelict. From Helebridge to the Harbour stopping up the towpath was not allowed under the Act, and this section was actively maintained for both Port and amenity purposes. This at times involved the Council, as Harbour authority, in considerable expense.

Early in the century a terrific storm in 1903, and a phenomenal high tide and heavy seas on 3rd February 1904 caused considerable damage to the breakwater and completely destroyed the lock gates, which were swept out to sea. A ketch the "Wild Pidgeon", moored just inside the gates, was also swept out to sea and became a total wreck under Summerleaze Point. She was owned by Mr N. Tregaskes, a Bude Merchant, but luckily there was no-one on board at the time. Another vessel, the "Jessie", broached across the now empty entrance and a large volume of water was released from the Canal.

The "Jessie" broached in the sea lock when it collapsed in 1904 due to a heavy gale

Canalside Activities

It is fair to say that the Bude Canal slipped into a "genteel retirement" in the inter war years of the 20's and 30's. Sea trade continued - ships berthed alongside a railway siding on the lower wharf which was part of the original scheme for 1898. Sand from the beach was taken up a slope and tipped directly into the railway trucks which enabled it to go further inland than ever before.

However, this traffic ceased in the 1940's but the siding continued to be used to bring coal and other goods to WW Petherick's store right up to 1964, only two years before the closure of the railway in 1966.

Henry Stapleton's shipyard on the upper wharf, founded in the 1850's, still flourished carrying out ship repairs, although this finally closed in 1917.

The steam saw-mills close by became the Bude Sanitary Laundry, where shirts and collars were redressed "equal to new" - a further feature being the "Open Air Drying Grounds". All this continued up to the second World War.

The main use of the Barge Canal was for amenity purposes administered by the Town Council. As early as 1906, Mrs Mary Stapleton is listed in Kelly's Directory as letting Rock Cottage (No. 2 Breakwater Road) for visitors also featuring "Pleasure boats for hire". This tradition, of course, carries on right up to the present day.

Between the wars the boat trips up the canal to Rodd's Bridge for a "cream tea" at the farm were a great feature of Bude's summer season.

The Lifeboat, with its solid Victorian house built in 1863 on the upper wharf, continued in service until 1923. It was supported of course, by traditional "Lifeboat Days" and Canal Sports. The Lifeboat was either launched into the canal and out through the sea lock, or through the other doors on a carriage pulled by 6 - 8 horses, to be trundled along the Strand and launched across Summerleaze Beach. The present inshore rescue boat house by the sea-lock gates was placed there in 1966 and opened by Mrs Rodgers, president of the local branch, who received the key from Councillor JH Maggs, Chairman of the Bude Stratton Urban Council, providers of the building.

It was dedicated by Canon Walter Prest, Vicar of Bude, with three crew members standing by - Coxswain Ken Cunningham, Michael Moyle and Ken Downing.

Over the inter-war years the Port Trade gradually died away, but vessels such as the famous ketch "Ceres" owned by the Petherick family of Bude, continued to bring in cargoes, mainly from South Wales and Ireland and taking, for example, barley to Scotland for the whisky distilleries. In 1884

The Twilight Years

Captain WW Petherick left the sea to take over his father's business and handed over command to his brother RW Petherick. "Captain Walter" spent 52 years in the "Ceres" from boyhood 'till retirement in 1928. A truly remarkable record in itself.

Getting in and out of Bude Haven was never easy and often dangerous. In storms or very high seas and swell conditions entrance to the harbour was quite impossible and vessels sometimes had to turn back or shelter in the lee of Lundy Island. All the vessels had to wait offshore until a flag was hoisted on Compass Point (by the "tide-waiter") indicating that the harbour could be entered.

Rarely did the ships enter the Haven without assistance from the hobblers (or hovellers) whose open rowing boat met them at the entrance to the channel to act as pilot and take ropes from the ship and occasionally to tow the boats right into the lock. Present members of the Petherick family can well remember going out in the hobblers boat and enjoying the return journey on board the 'Ceres' as she rounded Barrel Rock (the staff of which came from the propeller of the wrecked SS Belem) heading for the quay or the lock.

The appearance of masts in the lock was also a signal for children in the nearby school to rush out and get a free ride into the lower wharf basin.

The canal aqueduct over the river Tala Water near Druxton Wharf

After the 'Ceres sank off Baggy Point, North Devon, on the 25th November 1936, she was replaced by the steel-hulled ketch the 'Traly'.

We must not forget too the occasional visiting vessels. These included the steam yacht 'Fireflash' belonging to the Fry family of chocolate fame from Bristol. With their entourage, which included a large chow dog, they "seasoned" in Bude at Hartland House, now an hotel.

And what of the canal itself in these nostalgic twilight years? Inland (the "interior" as the surveyors called it) the canal became derelict, overgrown and in the main, forgotten. By the 1950's the Council was facing various problems. Under the law the whole 2 miles of canal from the sea lock to the bottom of the Marhamchurch inclined plane was still officially a navigable waterway, but the locks at Rodds Bridge and Whalesborough had been concreted since the 1920's. Also the Falcon Bridge was required to be maintained as a swing bridge, but had not been opened for forty years. At the same time, the cost of maintaining the obsolete Burmsdon aqueduct over the Tamar had necessitated the council borrowing money for repairs. Deliberations led to the presenting of a Bill to Parliament and the passing in 1960 of the Bude-Stratton Urban District Council Act. By this, the Council was empowered to dispose of the disused canal land from Helebridge to Vealand (excepted for Burmsdon Farm Bridge and the Tamar aqueduct), rights of navigation between Rodd's Bridge lock and Marhamchurch were extinguished (thus legalising the stopping of the locks) and the requirement that Falcon Bridge should be capable of being opened was removed. Within the next year or so sections of the disused length of canal from Helebridge to Vealand were sold, most being incorporated back into farm land. In 1967 Tamar Lake and the canal from it as far as Burmsdon were transferred to the North Devon Water Board. Thus, leaving only a 2 mile stretch from Bude in the ownership of the Bude-Stratton UDC The whole story went full circle when the railway - the "villain of the peace" - was itself closed in 1966.

The following year the Town Council announced that it too was taking steps to promote a private Bill through Parliament - "to secure the lock gates at the canal head, Bude, and replace them with a concrete weir and spillway". There was public uproar and the proposal was totally rejected. The working part of the canal lived on for another day.

A low-pitched store house at Blagdonmoor wharf

CHAPTER NINE
The Canal in 1998

Introduction

Although specifically described in the previous chapters the canal route covered in all 35½ miles through attractive, bleak, and sometimes remote private countryside which is not freely accessible to the public, but well worthy of being described in some detail. The Author was given permission to walk and photograph the whole length of the canal by local landowners and farmers, and privileged to follow in the footsteps of Monica Ellis, Helen Harris and Joan Rendell. Sometimes the canal disappears altogether, sometimes the towpath is a thick, thorn hedge, often the canal has been incorporated into the field alongside, and on many occasions, the canal bed is now a cart track. In places, the canal and towpath have become very overgrown and impassable which meant walking in the adjoining fields.

A superb example of an accommodation (farm) bridge at Haunch bridge, south of Boyton

Bude to Marhamchurch

The sea-lock, wharves and the 2 mile section to Helebridge are well known; there is an attractive walk from the Falcon bridge along a tarmac towpath past the locks at Rodds Bridge and Whalesborough. The river Neet supplies the water for this stretch - the canal and river run together for a short distance as far as the overflow weir.

Boating on the barge canal

The basin, wharf and store house at Helebridge

Points to Note
1. The turntable in the sand just beyond the iron bridge to the north of the sea-lock and the connecting railway to the sand wharf.
2. WW Petherick's coal yard is now a restaurant and Art Gallery.
3. The Wharf buildings beyond the old lifeboat house have been pulled down and a large block of flats has been built on what was once Sir Thomas Acland's wharf.
4. Milepost "Bude 1" beside the towpath near Rodds bridge.
5. The railway bridge at Helebridge has been demolished to make way for a new road bridge but the old road bridges over the canal and the river Neet still exist.
6. There is a small car park and picnic area to the south of the canal basin, and the old barge workshop has been restored as an open museum.
7. There is a right of way along the towpath and up the incline leading into the village. Box's Iron foundry, now a private house, is on the left half-way up the incline.

Marhamchurch to Vealand

The canal passes to the north of the village, crosses the Bude road (no bridge remains) and into what is now a development called appropriately "Old Canal Close". The old towpath is a right of way but soon comes to a dead end. At Court Farm the canal turns north - crosses a stream on an embankment, and for two or three fields has been obliterated before crossing the Stratton road (no bridge remains) into Cann Orchard farm. Here the canal, with water and mown towpath, is clearly visible. At the end, it crosses the Marsh-Hobbacott public road (bridge gone) and in the next field turns east to the base of the Hobbacott incline plane. It has been obliterated in the fields but in the woods is easily seen. At Thurlibeer farm the bridge has long gone but approaching Red Post the canal is visible but the towpath is a very thick thorn hedge. A hump in the main road (B3254) is all that remains before reaching the important junction with the Launceston Branch. The Canal takes a long one mile left-handed sweep around Shernick farm, where it can be followed quite easily, particularly from the farm to the Holsworthy road (A3072). The bridge over the farm lane has gone but there are two good examples of boundary stones in the farm porch. Skirting south of Anderton farm, the footings of a footbridge can be seen and although the canal has been levelled in the next field, it's an easy run into Burmsdon farm over a substantial embankment where the towpath is wide enough for farm vehicles. The well-preserved Burmsdon farm bridge and the famous Burmsdon aqueduct over the river Tamar follow, before the well-defined canal reaches the Vealand Inclined plane, now in the County of Devon. (See page 64).

Canal Close, Marhamchurch built on the canal bed

Points to Note
1. The recently opened up Adit or drain at the bottom of the Hobbacott plane with the two boat bays clearly visible.
2. The right of way from the main Stratton-Holsworthy road (A3072) only leads to the renovated cottage and does not go down the Incline, but eastwards across the valley to Hobbacott farm.
3. An old lay-bye on Shernick farm has been enlarged for coarse fishing.
4. The small bridge taking the track to Anderton farm has been doubled in size to take modern traffic.
5. The Vealand wheel-pit has been filled in but at the top of the plane are the old sand filter beds.

Vealand to Lower Tamar Lake (The feeder Arm and Reservoir)
The canal passes under the Vealand farm bridge to reach its "summit level". Hidden on the edge of a plantation behind Lishaperhill is the once important junction for the Holsworthy branch. A small distance further on

are the remains of a bridge used by horses and men changing towpaths. Brendon Bridge on the Lana - Puckland minor public road comes next which begins a four mile stretch of canal and towpath that is open to the public now being owned by the recently formed Bude Canal Trust. At Brendon bridge the footings have been strengthened and new railings and a gate have been built to allow access to this newly opened section of the canal. There is now a superb walk of one mile to Puckland Bridge where an exit/entrance to the towpath has been constructed with a short cleared pathway and a substantial wooden gate. There are three occupation bridges on this stretch - one 200 yards in, next Gainsmoor and finally Broomhill. All have new styles and wooden gates to allow easy access, plus a few other gates for animal control.

Puckland bridge has been rebuilt with wooden railings and on the north side there is a gate leading to the towpath, which is then a short walk to Morton Bridge and a cleared towpath to Dexbeer bridge. Godlock Bridge is followed by Wooda bridge where there is an old maintenance boat (14' 6" x 5') still stuck in the mud. After Aldercott bridge, Virworthy Mill (and wharf) is reached and a short distance further on is the end of the navigable part of the canal at Virworthy wharf and basin with its wharfinger's house and stables, now a private dwelling, and a renovated store house which houses excellent interpretation boards. The small feeder canal leads to the dam at the southern end of the 70 acre reservoir (Lower Tamar Lake) recently saved after a public outcry and is now strengthened. There is a car park for fishermen, birdwatchers and canal walkers.

Points to Note
1. The slots on the north side of Brendon Bridge into which planks were fitted as a "stop-lock" during repair work.
2. The unusual extra width of the canal near Gainsmore bridge.
3. The original cast-iron arches still in position on Morton Bridge.
4. The boundary store unusually marked "BHC 1840" (most are 1839) cemented into the towpath near Broomhill bridge.

Vealand to Holsworthy
The start of the Holsworthy branch can be seen just north of Highermoor Cross where it crosses the minor public road. The right-hand side is now a rubbish dump but it is possible to follow the canal beyond the dump until it comes to an abrupt end. At the back of Glebe cottage (ex Vicarage cottage) the canal and towpath disappear completely until reappearing amongst impassable scrub, saplings and trees. A high embankment follows which crosses a stream called "Small Brook". The culvert underneath is still intact

although there has been some erosion on the north side. The Thorne farm nature trail includes this attractive walk along the canal and is signposted from Burnards House on the main Holsworthy road (A3072). The canal then goes into a deep overgrown cutting before going under Thornemoor bridge - an excellent example of a "standard" canal designed bridge. In the next two fields the canal has been obliterated but can be identified in two woods before turning south marked by a thick trimmed hedge. There is an accommodation bridge, with a slit down the middle for the tow-rope, in the wood before the canal crosses the minor road ¼ mile north of Burnards House (See page 18). In the Parnacott Estate the canal has been levelled but can be identified by slight indentation in the ground before arriving at a lane leading to Parnacott House over which there is a right of way. The canal loops around Canal Farm, easily discernible though the wood and over an embankment with a culvert underneath carrying a small stream to the river Deer. Several boundary stones and mileposts can be seen in this area.

The canal and towpath at Hornacott Wood

There is no trace of the Canal bridge at the Chilsworthy - Holsworthy road but a public right of way follows the canal to the large Chilsworthy embankment which takes the canal over the river Deer. The embankment has been reduced in height but convenient steps have been made to allow the walker to reach North Hogspark. As the canal turns south it has been obliterated but the towpath appears on a high embankment at Higher Manworthy with a culvert underneath. As the canal approaches the Manworthy Mill road, it turns abruptly east and can be followed from the crossroads until it swings south across two open fields to Stanbury wharf beside the A388. The canal has been obliterated below Arscott farm. However, a thin line of trees and slight indentations in the ground shows the path to Blagdonmoor wharf, the end of the line, 1½ miles north east of Holsworthy.

Points to Note
1. Milepost 10 ½ on the Thorne Farm nature trail.
2. The footbridge in the wood near Burnards house has iron girders similar to Brendon Bridge.
3. There is no sign of the wharf in the farm lane leading S.E. from Parnacott .
4. The wharfinger's house at Stanbury wharf is still lived in and the old coal and sand store is now a shippon.

5. The weed filled basin at Blagdonmoor with a typical low pitched store house at the end. This wharf, like Stanbury wharf is now all private property but Stanbury wharf can be easily viewed from the Holsworthy - Bideford main road (A388).

The Launceston Branch - Red Post to North Tamerton

Without doubt, this branch of the canal is the most attractive and spectacular stretch of all and contains many excellent features that are well worth recording. It must also be one of the best kept secrets in North Cornwall! The first glimpse of the canal is in a fire break under the grid wires very close to the Launceston main (B3254) road a few hundred yards south of "Wayside" bungalow. In the next few fields the towpath is more pronounced than the canal and is very overgrown. In fact, it is used as a good hedge, especially in the field before the Buttsbeer cross - Treyeo lane where it is raised on a long embankment. After leaving the edge of Burn wood the canal arrives at the end of the Grove farm lane where it is built into the side of a steep hill with the river Tamar close by on the left. In order to keep to the 110 metre contour line, the canal swings right up the valley and doubles back, only to be obliterated where it crossed two large fields before going into a cutting, and with only the towpath visible, arrives at the Littlebridge aqueduct just west of Bridgerule. Little remains of the wharf but the buttresses can be seen on either side of the narrow road. After Borough Cross the towpath is visible but is obliterated near the Newacott road. From here the towpath is a thick unwalkable thorn hedge. Mile post 8 is still in the hedge. Merrifield descending incline plane runs down the back of Merrifield farm with its underground water-wheel pit at the top, one field in, and accessible.

The disused Bude railway line cuts through the canal at the base of the incline. From here to Druxton wharf the river Tamar is only yards from the canal, and at the next wood the Langaton leat runs between the river and the canal for the next ½ mile. Langaton Mill is now a private residence. The original mill having been used to build a shippon at the farm in 1890. From here to the Whitstone-Holsworhty road just south of Crowford bridge the canal starts in an open field marked with a wire fence and for the next ¼ mile is overgrown and in places impassable but easy to identify. It is then raised on a long embankment through the woods to cross a small stream before crossing the public road (no bridge remains). A service road made on the canal bed when a new line of Pylons was erected across East Balsdon farm allows easy walking until reaching open countryside. Here it disappears completely until the "hairpin" bend is negotiated. On the opposite hillside both canal and towpath are very overgrown but easily seen and holding water. Passing through a hunting gate, a farm gate and a

The Present State of the Canal

second hunting gate, an enjoyable walk begins around Haydon Farm through the woods. The old footings of a canal bridge can be seen before continuing through the delightful woods below Trepoyle farm. Just before coming to a large embankment with a culvert underneath, a "stop-lock" can be seen built into the stone sides of the canal. After crossing two fields where the canal has been levelled, its an easy walk through a line of majestic oak trees to North Tamerton (via the churchyard). The old wharf is now a cultivated sunken garden in a private residence (Haven cottage). The cottage was once a wharf store house for Bude sand. The wharfinger was housed in Wharf cottage beside the buttresses of the aqueduct that carried the canal across the public road.

Points to Note
1. The large quarry at the end of the Grove farm lane close to the canal.
2. The adit in the Merrifield pit is big enough to walk through.
3. Langaton farm is no longer open to the public.
4. In 1968 along this section mileposts 8, 11, 13, 13$^{1}/_{4}$, 13$^{1}/_{2}$, and 13$^{3}/_{4}$ were recorded.

North Tamerton to Druxton Wharf (Crossgate)
On the south side of the North Tamerton road is a canal store house, now a private bungalow (Canal Farm). It stored coal and wood and nearby are boundary and anchor stones. The canal continued through trees and shrubs behind Tamerton Town farm on a high steep bank to arrive at the top of the descending Tamerton Incline plane. The pit is dry and in good order (see page 42). The plane has been incorporated into the adjoining field. At the base of the incline the boat bays are still visible.

One of several locked hunting gates on the canal towpath

In Eastcott wood the canal and towpath can be easily followed until Underwood copse where it may be necessary to change sides for a short while. From the end of the Lower Hornacott farm track its an easy and delightful walk through Bradridge copse (Forestry Commission), and Bragshill wood to the Boyton road over a large curving embankment with a culvert underneath and onto the canal bed now a "Forestry" road.

Bradridge Little copse starts and ends with locked hunting gates but the towpath gives easy walking. The canal basin and towpath at Boyton can be easily identified but no wharf buildings remain. Three farm gates lead the way to Haunch bridge - a superior farm bridge similar to Burmsdon bridge. The canal here is cut out of solid rock, next to a working quarry. Around the next bend is the usual high curving embankment with a superb stone-faced culvert below, big enough to walk through. There is a four-rail style and a locked hunting gate leading to Colehill wood. The towpath opens out to a tractor-width track obviously used to go to the quarry and rubbish dump. Half-a-mile further on the canal leaves the farm track to curve right-handed before ending on a high ridge where an aqueduct crossed the public road at Tamertown. The buttresses can be seen and the canal follows the public road to the top of the Werrington incline plane with the wharfinger's house alongside still lived in, and there the plane drops down over the road. The canal follows the road just east of the two Bridgetown farms, and crosses Tala water with an aqueduct that was rebuilt in 1835 after severe flooding destroyed the original.

The canal and towpath leading into Devon from the Burmsdon aqueduct

The route crosses the road through a wood to the terminal basin - Druxton Wharf at Crossgate. Two company buildings remain in the grassed-over basin with the wharfinger's house near the road, which is still a residence today. And so ends a captivating and enchanting "journey" through some of the most attractive and remote countryside in North Cornwall - well worth placing on record for present and future generations.

Points to Note
1. How the canal was built into the solid rock face at the end of the lower Hornacott farm track and the sheer drop to the river Tamar very close by.
2. The anchor chain and boundary stone built into the garden wall of the bungalow beside the road where the canal crossed to the Boyton wharf area opposite. No trace of the bridge remains.
3. The adit in the underground wheelpit at Werrington is cut out of solid rock.

CHAPTER TEN

Into The Millennium

Over the past century the Bude Canal has remained in three distinct parts - The Barge Canal from Bude to Helebridge - The old feeder arm now known as the Bude Aqueduct from Lower Tamar Lake to Vealand and the remainder of the Tub-Boat system. The ownership patterns have not changed over much. Initially, the Barge Canal was taken over by the Stratton and Bude UDC. in 1902 and remained so for over 70 years. Eventually, it was handed over to the North Cornwall District Council in 1974 on the reorganisation of Local Government. This does mean that the two major "monuments" to the canal, the Sea-Lock and the Breakwater, are still firmly in local authority hands. The Aqueduct and Tamar lake, "Bude's Water Supply" initially, also belonged to the Town Council to be taken over by the North Devon Water Board and then sold to South West Water and subsequently to the North Cornwall District Council for a nature trail. The remainder of the canal system including the Incline planes, wheel pits, etc. has been sold back to the local landowners and farmers, many of whose ancestors had sold it to the Canal Company in the first place. This rather complex ownership pattern has meant that parts of the Bude Canal have at least been kept intact.

The high maintenance costs which had always plagued the old Bude Harbour and Canal Company are still very much with us. At the present time the Sea-Lock gates are virtually inoperable and grants are being sought to repair them. As has been mentioned, they had been a problem back in 1967 when the Town Council wanted to replace them with a concrete weir and spillway. These ever present maintenance problems led to the formation of the Bude Canal Society in 1990, it's aims being to see that the Bude Canal is preserved and that the public ownership pattern should continue. Another aim of the Society is to promote the canal through education and this has been achieved with lectures and slide shows. Numerous articles in newspapers and journals, both local and national, have advertised the existence of the canal far and wide. Guided walks have opened up knowledge of sections of the old canal which had become all but lost. Working in conjunction with the Canal Society has been the "Waterway Recovery Group", the restoration section of the Inland Waterways Associaiton. They have organised parties of dedicated volunteers to work on the Canal for a two week's camp in the summer months. Projects so far covered have included the strengthening of the Barge Canal banks and the installation of by-washes to Whalesbororugh and Rodds Bridge locks.

As early as 1993, moves were started by the District Council to dispose of some 5½ miles of the Bude Aqueduct from Tamar Lake which they still owned. The Bude Canal Society were to be the purchasers but before they could do this it was necessary for the Society to become a charitable trust limited by guarantee. This was achieved and the trust finally became the owners of the Aqueduct in 1996.

The Bude Canal Trust Ltd has been most successful in raising funding for the clearance of the Bude Aqueduct and its tow-path. This is now open and offers a splendid four mile walk from Brendon Bridge in Pancrasweek Parish to Lower Tamar Lake.

A "Social Section" of the Trust was established to carry on the fund raising activities. This group has now been dissolved and the "Bude Canal Society" has been reformed as an independent organisation. The wheel has turned full circle.

Another great problem has been the maintenance of the Tamar Lake Reservoir. For many years the lake had been Bude's water supply with water from the reservoir flowing along the aqueduct and then being piped to Bude from the Venn pumping works. As the town grew, so more and more water was needed. In 1976, the then Water Board built a further reservoir, "Upper Tamar Lake", more than doubling the water capacity. In the 90's problems began to appear with the Lower Lake's dam, and South West Water, the current owners then put forward a plan virtually to drain the lower lake. There was a public outcry and a protest campaign followed. South West Water relented and the dam was strengthened. The lake has been saved, at least for the time being.

Deep inside one of the adits at Hobbacott

And what of the future? There is a very strong body of opinion that the Bude Canal, a unique piece of Georgian West Country engineering, should be preserved as far as possible. The North Cornwall District Council have recently taken the initiative in seeking the funding for a firmly based strategic study as to exactly what the future restoration policy should be. As we approach the next Millennium the great pioneering spirit of the Bude Canal, now over 175 years old, lives on.

CHAPTER ELEVEN

The Regeneration Project

Project Beginnings

In 1995 the Bude Canal Society (BCS), as it then was, approached the North Cornwall District Council to raise concerns about the future of the Bude Canal. The primary aim of the BCS was to protect the heritage value of the canal and their principal fear was that it was beginning to degrade and that insufficient attention was being given to its long term existence. The part of the canal near Bude and still 'in water', which is owned by the District Council, is considered particularly important on account of the density of its early engineering features.

However, rapid silting, vegetation encroachment and the dereliction of key structures such as the inland locks were typical of what was seen as a disinterest which, if continued, would see the eventual disappearance of one of Cornwall's – perhaps the country's - most important historical canals.

The Council responded by encouraging the development of a Partnership of key local community groups and relevant statutory and non statutory organisations. Several Parish Councils, the Environment Agency, the Bude Angler's Association and the Town Council typified the range of organisations which were encouraged to join the group, which was chaired by District Councillor Neil Burden. The vision of the Partnership was to develop a plan for the restoration of the canal, to improve access to it and along it and to encourage a greater interest in it from the local community. By the end of the BCRP over 20 organisations were to be represented on the Partnership.

Thus it was that in 1997, with the encouragement of the Partnership underpinning events, a grant application was made to the South West Regional Development Agency (SWERDA) for a feasibility study to be undertaken to see what work was necessary to ensure the future of the canal.

Feasibility Studies

The early work was done by W.S. Atkins. In 1998 they delivered their report to the Partnership outlining what actions ought to be pursued in order to safeguard the canal and make it more of a focal point for Bude. The report came up with 10 recommendations, the main one being the need to put the canal back into operational use. This would require, as a minimum, a comprehensive dredging of the canal and the restoration of the disused locks at Rodd's Bridge and at Whalesborough.

The Partnership set about encouraging the local community to participate in the development of these ideas. A consultation process took place on the recommendations of the Atkins report and there was enough evidence of public support to enable the Partnership to progress another stage of assessing more detailed feasibility and identifying costs.

Consequently a further engineering and economic feasibility study was commissioned, again assisted by funding from the South West Regional Development Agency. This time Halcrow were selected to undertake the work and their report, published in 2001, looked specifically at how the restoration works could be undertaken and what would be required to implement the other key elements of the Atkins report. It also identified the likely costs of the works.

A wider public opinion was now sought through a full consultation process which again demonstrated the presence of great support and helped to secure the continuance of grant funding. Following the event the analysis of the consultation process led the Partnership to decide that the project was truly viable and that further staff resources should be obtained to prepare more detailed proposals and specifications for each element of the identified project objectives.

In 2004 contact was made with the Heritage Lottery Fund which encouraged the Partnership to apply for HLF assistance in two phases. The first, a Development Phase, would enable details of the project to be set out and for specialist civil engineering consultants to be engaged to produce drawings and specifications which would be used as a means of identifying the full cost of the project and how each element could be managed.

In addition the amount of the grant support for this phase, for which the application was being made, would allow the employment by the District Council of specialist dedicated staff to help deliver the detailed work required and prepare the evidence of public support necessary to source the funds for implementing the project. This implementation, if all was successful, would form the second phase.

The reconsruction of Rodd's Bridge lock

Simultaneously grant applications were submitted to SWERDA, which continued to be very supportive of the project, and also for European funds under the European Regional Development Fund "Objective 1" programme.

The Development Phase

In March 2005 a sum of £271,000 was approved for a first phase of the project. Within a few months Ian Mander, a chartered civil engineer, and Andrea Vaillancourt-Alder, an educationalist with experience of a community development programme allied to another canal restoration scheme, were appointed to take forward the Development Phase of the project.

The new lock gates at Rodd's Bridge

By March 2006 the Bude Canal team, guided by the Partnership, had prepared plans for the project encompassing Engineering, Conservation, Business, Interpretation, Audience Development and Educational, Access, Marketing and Training matters. These plans formed the substantive basis on which the funding organisations would decide whether to approve grant aid towards what they were suggesting was a very ambitious project! More months of detailed communications with the funding organisations then followed and a detailed three volume report was presented to HLF.

The outcome was successful! In October 2006 project funds were secured for the Implementation Phase which amounted to about £3.5 million. The HLF approved a contribution of £1.6m, ERDF investments from "Objective 1" to just over £1 million and SWERDA agreed a further lift to their contributions by £600 000. North Cornwall District Council contributions and the pledges by others from within the Partnership topped up the funding available to just over £3.8 million.

At the same time as all this was happening the District Council, in partnership with Devon County Council in whose area a significant portion of the historic canal lies, had been awarded a grant through another of the European programmes to develop walking routes along inland lengths of the canal. This complemented the BCRP well with an opportunity to make improvements in access to the several original branches of the canal on a much wider front.

The Implementation Phase

By the end of October 2006 Ian and Andrea had been reappointed for the Implementation Phase and the work now started in earnest. There was a deadline for completion of 31st December 2008, a significant date when the ERDF funding programme for Cornwall was due to end. Work carried over into 2009 might not be eligible for a portion of the grants allocated – a definite incentive to complete on time!

The Bude Canal Regeneration Partnership was restructured and a wider participation invited. A constitution was developed. The Partnership remit remained one of overseeing the broader objectives of the project, but to enable the expanded Partnership to maintain a close involvement with rapidly moving developments it was agreed that a small Steering Group would be constituted to oversee the more immediate works in hand. The Partnership met three times a year but the Steering Group every month. Neil Burden was re-elected Chairman and elected Chairman of the Steering Group.

Work was divided into defined contract areas, targeting different construction specialities. The project team initially concentrated on managing the preparation of the contract drawings and specifications and finalising required permissions such as getting Planning, Flood Defence and Building Control consents in place. The first construction contract was awarded in February 2007 for the fresh re-surfacing and a new "urban landscaping" of the Lower Wharf area: this would see the previous predominantly car parking area transformed into a more pedestrian-friendly wharf enabling better access to and views of what is an important historic location in Bude. The contract was awarded to roads and surfacing specialists CORMAC, and was valued at £550,000.

The rest of the contract awards followed on behind. The work on the canal more inland was seldom easy though: there was the challenge of getting access into the narrow corridor of the canal which stretches along the edge of the floodplain, for the major construction plant required for dredging of the canal and for repairing and re-building structures, banks and paths. It may be easier for the future now that the locks can be used and the canal is navigable!

The most challenging contract preparation task covered the restoration of the locks since there were many unknowns within the old structures. It had not been feasible to explore fully into the depth of these structures during the Development Phase and so preparing a suitable contract specification in the absence of this knowledge was a cause of much thought.

In the end nine main contracts would be awarded in order to complete the Implementation Phase. These works covered the hard urban landscaping, soft landscaping, buildings, locks refurbishment and canal dredging, banks and towpath improvements, bridge modifications, landing stages, sculptures, seating and various elements of canal interpretation, guidance and safety for users and visitors.

March 2008 Bude Sea Lock storm damage

As if all the work to be done on the main line of the canal wasn't enough, on the evening of March 10th 2008 a north-westerly storm event coincided with one of the highest tides of the year. The huge waves and swell generated by the storm entered the sea lock, caught the southern of the two timber lock gates under its cross members and lifted it off its hinges. Each time a big wave entered the lock it moved the gate further askew allowing water from the harbour to start to drain out to sea as the tide ebbed.

To prevent total loss of the water from the canal from the sea lock upstream as far as Rodd's Bridge lock a coffer dam was hurriedly built on the upstream side of the Falcon Bridge. This was critical. The consequence of failing to prevent the canal water escaping to the sea was that all of the fish would have perished, the outdoor activity businesses would have lost income and damage may have been caused to the banks of the canal through the loss of the support provided by the water.

The coffer dam used 120 dumpy bags each containing about 1 cubic meter of sand or stone. The dam was largely completed by 2.00am early on the morning of March 11th. Local contractors and building suppliers rallied around to help the Council by opening up their depots and bringing in machinery to enable the work.

Once the main Lower Wharf basin was drained and the south gate removed for repairs, the District Council took the decision to undertake repairs to the basin and its structures which the loss of water had revealed. These repairs were quite extensive and included a requirement to dredge the basin of some 6,000 cubic meters of silt, which would allow deeper keeled boats to access the harbour once again. The major part of the rest of the work was the stabilisation of the harbour and canal side walls.

Speed was essential, with the busy summer period approaching. Using local engineering consultants, John Grimes, and drafting in technical assistance from the neighbouring Caradon District Council, North Cornwall District Council was quickly in a position to appoint CORMAC to undertake the works. These works were completed by the end of the agreed contract period, June 30th 2008.

It had been anticipated that the Lower Basin would take a week to refill; the coffer dam was being slowly removed to allow a gentle flow of replenishing water. However on the day of the ceremony, arranged to mark the end of the contract and the beginning of the refilling, July 8th, there was such a storm inland that a surge of water came down the canal knocking out the coffer dam and causing the Lower Basin to refill completely within 4 hours! Providence!

The cost to the District Council however, as no grant was available for the Lower Basin work, was just under £500,000. This included some structural changes to the sea lock gates so that, in similar circumstances as were experienced in March, the gates would not be affected in the same way.

Contracts

The storm of the 8th July typified the weather during the main construction period of the summer of 2008. Often damp and raining, with soggy ground and regular spates of water down the canal, the work on the inland lock gate restoration, bank repairs and the dredging of the canal was challenging and laborious.

The dredging of the entire length of the canal from Helebridge to Falcon Bridge was attempted initially by pumping slurry to a disposal site on the neighbouring farm, but the distance and the 'lift' required from the pumps to reach the high, stony ground where the waste would best benefit the soil was very challenging. Later, as the advancing front of the dredging extended the pipe line beyond a practicable capability, barges took over moving the dredged material back up the canal to a transfer point and a final disposal by overland haulage. This applied to all the dredging in the length from Rodd's Bridge to Falcon Bridge.

Some 17,000 cubic metres (25,000 tons) of dredged material was taken out of the canal and deposited on adjacent farmland where it is incorporated into the soil and acts as a soil conditioner. Extensive analyses and the permissions from regulatory bodies were prerequisites for this to be allowed.

Contracts had to be run simultaneously giving rise to some interesting balancing by the project managers; it is never ideal to have two different contractors working in the same place. A good example was that the dredging company needed the water levels high at all times to float their barges whilst the contractor

Dredging the lower basin in 2008.

undertaking bank stabilisation wanted the water level low to enable them to get to the bottom of the banks they were working on.

As a justification for grant aid the Regeneration Project needed to provide significant economic benefits to the Bude area. For this reason the project included the construction of four new canal-side workshops on the Lower Wharf and four new office spaces above the new visitor centre. It was the intention that the occupants of the workshops would be craft based and that the activities they undertook added interest to those enjoying the public open space the Lower Wharf now provides. The design of the workshops reflected the industrial heritage of the area, each individually designed with a wharf-side character.

In tandem with the engineering works a contract was prepared and let to undertake the fitting out of the newly constructed Visitor Centre. The District Council agreed to fund the revamping of the existing Tourist Information Centre at the same time so that there was a seamless join between the two and each element gelled together. This facility was always seen as the focus point for people who wanted to find out more about the canal. An educational room was also provided to enable visiting school groups to use the canal as a learning resource.

As December 31st 2008 drew closer all efforts were concentrated on trying to get as many of the contracts completed as possible so that the Council could ensure it drew down from the European ERDF grant to the maximum amount available.

The projects were substantially completed by the end date, although the HLF did agree an extension to the end of March 2009, co-incidentally the same date on which the grant applicant, NCDC, ceased to exist as it was subsumed into the single new council for Cornwall.

The Bude Canal Regeneration Project was always an ambitious plan and the scope of the project had to be reduced during the Development Phase in order to pitch the bids for grants at acceptable levels. As a result, at the end of the Implementation Phase of the project some key elements are still an aspiration - required to fulfil the early vision of the Regeneration Partnership but yet to be initiated. These include the raising of Rodd's Bridge to allow an air draught of 2.2 meters or more, the reconnection of the canal at Helebridge to the Helebridge Wharf and the provision of a slipway at each end of the canal to allow boats to launch into it. These elements will be pursued by the Partnership with the new Council and it is hoped in due course will be completed and thus add significantly to the value of an already substantial achievement.

Main Contracts

Contract	Contractor	Date	Cost
Lower Wharf	Cormac (Eastern)	March 2007	£552k
Lower Wharf Basin	Cormac (Eastern)	March 2008	£500k
Workshops	Pearce Construction	July 2007	£516k
Visitor Centre build	J & E Reagan	Sept 2007	£251k
Locks/Dredging	South West Highways	Sept 2007	£1.3m
Interpretation	20/20	March 2008	£200k
Towpath renewal	Dyer & Butler	Sept 2008	£300k
A39 underpass	Cormac (Eastern)	June 2008	£125k
Helebridge wharf	Cormac (Eastern)	June 2008	£110k
Burmsdon Bridge	Calweton	August 2008	£90k

Project Management
Regeneration Partnership and Steering Group Chairman: Neil Burden (NCDC)*
Project Director: Charlie David (NCDC)
Project Manager: Ian Mander (NCDC)
Community Development Manager: Andrea Vaillancourt-Alder (NCDC)
Assistant Project Managers: Keith Field (NCDC), Steve Blatchford (CDC)*
Ken Bouch (NCDC), Julian Urbans (CCC)*
Clerk of Works: Brett Higham (NCDC), Martin Wherry (CCC)

Project Steering Group
North Cornwall District Council: Cllr Neil Burden, Cllr Val Newman
Bude Canal and Harbour Society: Audrey Wheatley, Bryan Dudley Stamp
Inland Waterways Assn. West Country Branch: Mike Moore, Chris Jewell
Bude Canal Trust: Mike Selby-Heard, Gerald Fry, Tim Dingle
Cornwall County Council: Bob Booker,
Devon County Council: Steve Church
Pancrasweek Parish Council: Mick Stanton
Marhamchurch Parish Council: Michael Grills
Bude Stratton Town Council: Town Clerk
South West Lakes Trust: Laurence Coldrick
Bude Angler's Association: Dick Turner
Boat Boatmen's Association: Len Benson
Bude Partnership: Lucille Opie

Principal Contractors
South West Highways (Exeter):Locks, Dredging and towpath works

J & E Regan (Saltash): Visitor Centre extension
Pearce Construction (Barnstaple): Workshop new build/Bark House repair
Cormac (Eastern) (Bodmin): Lower Wharf pedestrianisation, A39 underpass, Lower Wharf basin repairs, Helebridge basin works
Dyer and Butler: Towpath and bank stabilisation
Calweton: Burmsdon Aqueduct restoration
20/20: Visitor Centre interpretation and TIC refit

Main sub contractors
Knowle Plant (Bude): Ground works, towpath, Whalesborough Bridge
Blue Boar Contracts Ltd (Rugby): Dredging
Martin Childs Ltd (Cambridge): Lock Gates

Principal Consultants
Pre-Development Phase: Halcrow Group Ltd, Exeter, W. S. Atkins, Exeter & Cardiff
Development and Implementation Phases: PDP Green Consulting, Camborne; Scott Wilson Ltd, Plymouth; John Grimes Partnership Ltd, Ivybridge

*NCDC - North Cornwall District Council, CDC - Caradon District Council, CCC - Cornwall County Council

The empty Lower Wharf after storm damge to the lock gates.

Appendix I

VIEWING POINTS: Ordnance Survey 1:50,000 series sheet 190, Bude and Clovelly.

Sea Lock to Helebridge
1. Sea-Lock, sand railway, upper and lower basins and Falcon bridge.
2. 1st Lock at Rodds bridge and 2nd lock at Whalesborough.
3. Helebridge wharf area, old storehouse and towpath.
3a. Marhamchurch incline plane and Engineer's house.

Helebridge to Vealand
4. Marhamchurch - Stratton road. "Old Canal Close" built on canal bed towpath is a right of way.
5. Cann Orchard farm. Clear view of canal from road.
6. South of Red Post - hump in main road (B3254).

Vealand to Holsworthy
7. Just north of Highermoor Cross, canal crossed road.
8. Just north of Burnard's House, canal crossed road.
9. Thorne Farm Nature Trail travels over large Canal embankment.
10. Chilsworthy - Holsworthy road - Towpath is right of way to Hogs Park over the Chilsworthy canal embankment.
11. Manworthy Cross - Canal runs alongside road.
12. Stanbury Wharf, Wharfinger's cottage and warehouse can be viewed from main road (A388).
13. Blagdonmoor wharf - warehouse and basin. Whole area now private property.

Vealand to Lower Tamar Lake (the Bude Aqueduct)
14. Brendon Bridge - entrance to newly opened towpath to the lower lake.
15. Puckland bridge - entrance/exit to newly opened towpath.
16. Moreton bridge - with original cast iron arches.
17. Dexbeer bridge - part of the walk from Lower Tamar lake.
18. Virworthy Wharf - basin and ex-warehouse, now with interpretation boards.
19. Lower Tamar Lake - embankment/dam - start of walk south - car park.

Red Post to Druxton Wharf - The Launceston Branch

20. Littlebridge aqueduct - footings only.
21. Borough Cross - Bridgerule road - towpath now hedge.
22. Merrifield Incline - from far end of old railway station.
23. South of Crowford bridge - towpath and canal visible from minor road.
24. North Tamerton - Holsworthy road - footings of aqueduct and wharfinger's house and storehouse (now a bungalow).
25. Boyton-Chapman's Well road - well marked towpath and basin.
26. Tamartown - footings of aqueduct either side of minor road.
27. Werrington Incline plane - incline over road, with the keeper's house visible at the top.
28. Bridge over Tala water - view of aqueduct.
29. Bridgetown - crossgate road - canal crossed road into wood.
30. Druxton Wharf - wharfinger's cottage, warehouse and basin visible from road. All private property.

The canal and towpath at Cann Orchard

The wharfinger's house at Stanbury wharf

A store house at Druxton wharf

A culvert and free-standing wall protecting the maintenance track at Hornacott

Appendix II

Ships built at Bude

The upper basin of the Bude Canal provided a safe launching site for ships built or repaired at the port of Bude. They were brought out and launched broadside on at Stapleton's boatyard and numerous other ships were lengthened, rerigged, or repaired, and in many cases, such as the 'Ceres', replanked as good as new. Even before the Canal was constructed the Brig 'Mary' was built by Williams Barrow and launched from the beach in 1813. She was lost off the French coast in 1834.

Date	Ship	Owner/Masters	Fate
1826	Sloop Friends	Built and owned by Thomas Round. Master: W Whitefield	Lost at sea 1851.
1828	Sloop Enterprise	Built and owned by Thomas Round	Sold to new owners at Portsmouth 1830.
1835	Ketch Lady Acland	Davey-Elliott-Wonnacott	-
1836	Sloop Affo	Beer-Gorman-Drew	Wrecked Hartland 1871
1837	Sloop Victoria	Not known	Not known
1842	Sloop Mirre	Pickard-Bate	Wrecked 1875
1842	Sloop Velocity	Not known	Not known
1857	Schooner Elizabeth Scown	Lashbrook-Elliott-Sluggett	Wrecked Bude 1877
1861	Ketch Sir T Acland	Whitefield-Hallett	Not known
1865	Schooner Ellen Martin `(repaired)	W. Maynard	Wrecked Bude 1873

Date	Ship	Owner/Masters	Fate
1872	Schooner Annie Davey	W. Stone-Howell	Wrecked Bude 1899
1877	Ketch Jessamine	W Maynard	Lengthened in 1896. End unknown
1878	Schooner Agnes	Rowland	Lost in blizzard 1891
1903 (rebuilt completly)		Ketch Lady Acland	Bought by Edward Rudland and named Margaret Frances, then bought by Mr Tregaskes who renamed her Agnes after a previous Agnes built in 1835 and wrecked in 1873. Masters-Davey-Elliott-Wonnacott-Barrett.

Above Left:
The launch of "Annie Davey" at Stapleton's shipyard, 1873

Below Left:
The launch of the "Lady Acland ("Agnes"), 1903

79

Appendix III

Summary of Facts

The total length of the canal as built was thirty five and a half miles in three sections

    i. Wide Barge Section   Bude to Helebridge
    ii. Narrow Tub Boat Section   Helebridge to Blagdonmoor Wharf (Holsworthy) with a branch to Druxton (Launceston)
    iii. The Aqueduct   Tamar Lake reservoir to Burmsdon

Locks
    i. Bude Sea Lock (with breakwater)
    ii. Rodd's Bridge Lock
    iii. Whalesborough Lock

Inclined Planes - six, in place of locks

i.	Marhamchurch	120ft rise	836ft long
ii.	Hobbacott Down (Thurlibeer)	225ft rise	935ft long
iii.	Vealand	58ft rise	500ft long
iv.	Merrifield	60ft fall	360ft long
v.	Tamerton	59ft fall	360ft long
vi.	Werrington (Bridgetown)	51ft fall	259ft long

Date of start of construction: 23rd July 1819
Date of final completion: 1825
Final abandonment of works: 1901

List of Ships and Masters from page 45

On Left		*On Right*	
"Elizabeth"	W Brinton	"Friendship"	A Stephens
"Sir T D Acland"	G Hallett	"Ant"	H Hines
"Purveyor"	H Rooke	"Brackley"	Morgan
"Tavy"	H Mountjoy	"Joseph & Thomas"	B Shazell
"Hawk"	F Martin	"Stucley"	W Cook
"Lady Acland"	E Cunningham	"Wild Pigeon"	G Barrett
"Boconnoc"	W Sluggett	"Ceres"	R W Petherick
"Kindly Light"	J B Cook	"Du I Win"	J Chidgey

Acknowledgements

We would like to thank Monica Ellis and Joan Rendell who gave us such help with research material.

We would also like to thank the Bude Canal Trust, Social Section, (now the Bude Canal Society) for their encouragement and financial grant that started the writing of this book.

To the curators of the Bude Town Museum, Harvey and Gill Kendall, for the loan of their large selection of slides.

To Pam Williams who did all the typing so efficiently.

To Tim Martindale for the design and helpful advice in producing this book.

Bibliography

"Along the Bude Canal" by Joan Rendell.
"The Story of the Bude Canal" by Joan Rendell.
"Walking along the Old Bude Canal" by Bill Young.
"The Bude Canal" by Helen Harris and Monica Ellis.
"The Canals of South West England" by Charles Hadfield.
"The History of the Bude Canal" by Marcus Newman.

Illustration Acknowledgements

Authors' collections except:
Town Museum (ex Denis Jury collection):
Pages 8, 9, 10, 13, 17, 23, 25, 31, 33, 34 (RT), 45, 47, 50, 52 (lower), 53, 71
Mrs J Gliddon:
Page 29
Tim Martindale:
Pages 30, 35 (upper). 36, 37, 38 (lower), 42, 83, back cover (bottom)
Ken Bennett (founder member of the Bude Canal Society):
Page 67
John Stedwell:
Pages 12, 20, 26, 49, 58
Ross Hoddinott:
Front cover, back cover (top), page 75,
NCDC: Pages 68, 69, 72

The Authors

Bill Young was born at East Chinnock, near Yeovil, and educated at Crewkerne Grammar School. He joined the Royal Air Force on 16th May 1938 on a short service commission as an Acting Pilot Officer. After training he was posted to RAF Cleave - target towing with Westland Wallace Aircraft, and graduated to Hawker Henleys, Hurricanes and Defiants. After a short spell on Fighter Reconnaissance Mustangs with No 4 Sqn. he was posted to India for three years. He qualified as a flying instructor and completed his regular service in 1971. Since then he has written books on Walking the Bude Canal, and with Bryan Dudley Stamp, Bude Past and Present. He has also made three videos with John Street on Bude Lifeboats, the Bude Canal, and the Bude Railway.

Bryan Dudley Stamp was born in Ashtead, Surrey in the '20s - just. He first came to Bude on holiday in 1938 so experienced at first hand the 'Golden Years'. He has lived here ever since travelling to London by train! After National Service he studied at McGill University in Canada coming out with an honours degree in geography. He became a land agent working in London until his father's death in 1966. He is interested in all things Bude: currently the secretary of the Bude Canal and Harbour Society. Previous works include: The Book of Bude and Stratton with Rennie Bere published in 1980 and Bude Past and Present with Bill Young published in 1996.